Enchanted Childhoods

Other Books by Shirley Sargent

Pioners in Petticoats, 1966
Father of Forestry: Theodore Parker Lukens, 1969
John Muir in Yosemite, 1971
Yosemite and Its Innkeepers, 1975
The Ahwahnee Hotel, 1977, revised edition 1990
Yosemite's Historic Wawona, 1979
Galen Clark: Yosemite Guardian, 1981
Yosemite's Rustic Outpost. Foresta-Big Meadow, 1983
Dear Papa. Letters Between John Muir and His Daughter Wanda, 1985
Yosemite, A National Treasure, 1988
Solomons of the Sierra: The Pioneer of the John Muir Trail, 1989

Books edited by Shirley Sargent

Mother Lode Narratives, 1970
    by Jessie Benton Fremont
A Summer of Travel in the High Sierra, 1972
    by Joseph N. LeConte
A Western Journey With Mr. Emerson, 1980
    by James Brantley Thayer
Seeking The Elephant, 1849, 1980
    by James M. Hutchings

Enchanted Childhoods

Growing Up In Yosemite, 1864-1945

Shirley Sargent

Flying Spur Press   Yosemite, California

Cover design by Larry Van Dyke

Printed in the United States of America

Publisher's Cataloging in Publication
(Prepared by Quality Books Inc.)

Sargent, Shirley
    Enchanted childhoods : growing up in Yosemite, 1864–1945 / by
Shirley Sargent
    p. cm.
    Includes biographical references and index.
    Preassigned LCCN: 93–70281.
    ISBN: 1–878345–23–0
    1. Yosemite National Park (Calif.)—Biography. 2. Children—
Yosemite National Park (Calif.)   I. Title. II. Title: Growing up
in Yosemite, 1864–1945.

F868.Y6S37 1993   979.4'47'092
                                          QBI93–20143

Flying Spur Press • P.O. Box 278 • Yosemite, CA 95389

This book is dedicated to the memory of
Leroy J. Rust,
known to legions of friends as Rusty.
His lifelong devotion to Yosemite,
where he was born in 1920
and died in 1992,
was exceeded only by
his blithe and infectious spirit.

Contents

Introduction   ix

Yosemite Valley Tomboys   1
Camping in Yosemite   8
Yosemite School Days   11
Wawona Boyhood, 1884–1900   20
Childhood of Enchantment, 1894–1910   24
Village Youths   35
In the Footsteps of John Muir   46
The 1920s   57
A Decade of Changes   70
The Great Flood   81
Tuolumne Tomboy   91
Yosemite at War   97

Sources   107
Index   111

Introduction

SEVERAL YEARS AGO, when I first envisioned this book, I saw it as an anthology of narratives by people who had grown up in Yosemite, and who later in life had recorded the perspectives and perceptions gained from living in that spectacular place. For starters, I could quote from hotelkeeper's daughter Marjorie Cook Wilson, whose unpublished autobiography was in the Yosemite Research Library, and from autobiographical articles by Laurence V. Degnan that had been published in a Yosemite journal. Jay C. Bruce's book *Cougar Killer* contained several pages about his childhood in Wawona, and Mary Curry Tresidder had penned some reminiscences of her younger years at Camp Curry. And, I thought, there would be others.

But there weren't others—only fragmentary memoirs existed, and they were unorganized, scattered, sometimes almost indecipherable. Taped recordings weren't much more helpful, since the topics were rarely related to childhood. Although an anthology didn't seem to be feasible, and my notes had burned, I determined to put together what I could, solicit the "oldtimers" of this century, and organize the material into chapters.

After I had begun, I discovered that a reunion of people who had attended Yosemite Elementary School was being planned. Even though my enrollment there in 1941 had been short, I qualified as an alumna, and I quickly became involved with the plans.

That led me to request reminiscences and insights from more than fifty alumni on their youthful experiences in Yosemite. It is their responses that so enliven the final chapters, on what we all agreed were enchanted childhoods.

Acknowledgments to those many generous individuals who aided me would resemble a telephone directory, beginning with A for Adams (Anne, Michael, and Virginia), and ending with Z for Zaepffel. Indeed, I am indebted to almost every person, dead and alive, named in the index at the end of this book, and believe me, their help was and is appreciated.

Some people deserve special acknowledgment because I called on them so often. Both Linda Eade and Jim Snyder, respectively the librarian and the curator for the Park Service's Yosemite Research Library, provided me with written material, photographs, maps, and encouragement throughout my work. Virginia Best Adams, Stewart Cramer, Mary Degen Rogers, Anne Adams Helms, Pat Phillips Kessler, Alan Haigh, John Osborne, Keith Walklet, Leroy Radanovich, Ingrid Ringrose, and George McLean deserve mention. Peter Browning's judicious editing and his publishing and computer expertise, Janet Griffin-Langley's typing and retyping, and Helen Fowler's eye and shoulder also assisted, as did Alice Milldrum, whose suggestions, ideas, and meals were excellent. Larry Van Dyke designed the eye-catching cover, and thus deserves my gratitude. My thanks to everyone listed—and my apologies to anyone inadvertently missed.

SHIRLEY SARGENT

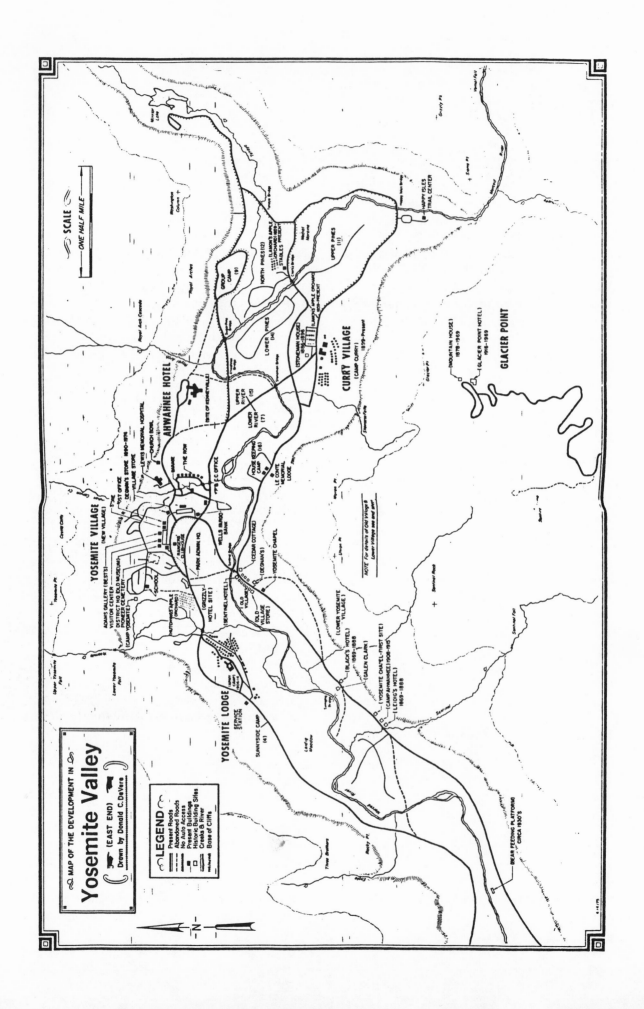

🦋 MAP OF THE DEVELOPMENT IN 🦋

Yosemite Valley

(EAST END)

Drawn by Donald C. DeVere

🦋 LEGEND 🦋

Present Roads
Abandoned Roads
No Auto Access
Present Buildings
Historic Building Sites
Creeks & River
Base of Cliffs

SCALE

ONE HALF MILE

1

Yosemite Valley Tomboys

UNTOLD GENERATIONS of Native Americans were born in Yosemite before whites began living in Yosemite Valley in the late 1850s, but no white child was born there until 1864. Florence Hutchings was delivered in the morning of August 24 of that year. Within a few years, Florence proved to be the most flamboyant child ever to grow up in that wonderland, and at age seventeen became only the third non-native child to die and be buried in Yosemite Valley.

Her multitalented and controversial father, Englishman James Mason Hutchings, had recorded several firsts himself. In 1855 he had organized and led the first tourist party to visit Yosemite, and from then until his death, while entering the Valley in 1902, he was its first and most prominent publicist.

Among his notable contributions to California literature were "The Miners' Ten Commandments," most of the articles in his *California Magazine* (1856–61), and three books: *Scenes of Wonder and Curiosity in California*, *In the Heart of the Sierras*, and *Souvenir of California*.

Four months before Florence's birth in 1864, Hutchings had begun hotelkeeping in a twenty-by sixty-foot, two-story inn called, because of its location, the Upper Hotel, but which was soon renamed Hutchings House. In it he installed his dreamy, pregnant wife, Elvira, who, at age twenty-one was twenty-two years his junior, and her competent and capable mother, Florantha Sproat, who was only ten years older than her son-in-law. Florence, commonly called Floy, became the third female in the somewhat disorganized household. As innkeepers, her parents had scant time to give Floy attention. Even her no-nonsense grandmother was too busy cooking and housekeeping to give Floy consistent direction. Not surprisingly, her behavior was unconventional.

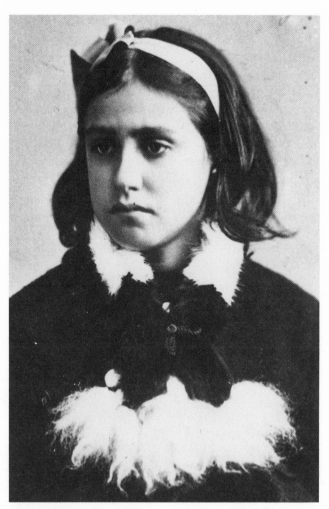

Florence Hutchings, a fearless and impulsive tomboy, was the first white child born in Yosemite and the third one to die there. (Yosemite Research Library Collection. YRL)

Tourist season coincided with the waterfalls' glory, beginning early in April and diminishing in July. After that, patronage was insignificant, Bridalveil Fall becoming slender and Yosemite Falls a trickle if not entirely dry. As the days shortened, so did the sunlight on the cliff-shaded south side of the valley. During winter, less than two hours a day of sun lit the barn-like hotel, and, despite the surrounding beauty, it was gloomy and depressing. Hutchings, aided by fellow pioneer James Lamon, built a comfortable log cabin, with good-sized windows to let in all available sunlight, on the north side of the Valley. A large fireplace heated the living room, a bedroom, and even the attic. A lean-to on the back housed a kitchen, presided over by Mrs. Sproat, plus a storeroom. Hutchings' large library "of nearly eight hundred volumes," he said, was shelved in the parlor, and his ever-growing collection of photographs, paintings, pine cones, and curios festooned the walls.

In the evenings, while Elvira and her mother sewed or knit in front of the fire, Hutchings read aloud. Consequently Floy was lulled to sleep by the classics and by what her father termed "the grandest of all anthems from Yosemite Falls."

During daytime Floy could chatter to Sultan, a parrot who soliloquized "in Arabic and Hindostanee," or could admire the pet grosbeak. On walks with her mother she learned to identify trees, flowers, cliffs, and waterfalls. Wild animals were rarely seen, because most meadows were fenced and full of horses and cattle.

Inevitably the perceptive child absorbed a deep appreciation and love of the unique environment. Once tourist season began, Floy busied herself climbing boulders, making mud pies, and playing games around the hotel.

Florence's early education was haphazard, diverse, and not always refined. She was a precocious three when photographer Eadweard Muybridge taught her to say "I used to smoke a meerschaum, but now I smoke a 'torn tob.'" People laughed then, but years later were scandalized, as she meant them to be, to see her puff on a pipe.

Muybridge was among the score of hotel guests that Hutchings claimed offered "elevating companionship," because they were "eminent in letters, in science, and in art." Among these were Ralph Waldo Emerson, James A. Garfield, William Keith, Joseph LeConte, and Helen Hunt Jackson.

Wallpaper and Yosemite memorabilia lined the walls of James Hutchings' log cabin. At night he sat in the armchair he had made from manzanita wood, while reading aloud from one of his eight hundred books. (YRL Collection)

In 1868 poet Charles Warren Stoddard spent part of the winter with the Hutchings family in their cabin. "O, halcyon days," he wrote in remembrance, "and bedtime at eight p.m., tucking in for ten good hours and up again at six; good eatings and drinkings, mugs of milk and baked squash forever, plenty of butter to our daily bread."

Floy's early independence and fearlessness were recorded. "Such a queer little child," Stoddard wrote, "left to herself, no doubt thinking she is the only little one in existence, contented to teeter for hours on a plank by the woodpile, making long explorations by herself and returning, when we are all well frightened, with a pocketful of lizards and a wasp in her fingers; always talking of horned toads and heifers; not afraid of snakes, not even the rattlers; mocking the birds when she is happy, and growling bear-fashion to express her disapproval of any thing."

After her sister's birth in October of 1867, Floy was not so solitary. Although christened Gertrude for the ship that had carried her father from England to America, the "precious darling of a child" was enduringly nicknamed "Cosie." In time she became a companion to Flo and developed an independence of her own. William Mason Hutchings, born in August 1869, completed the family. Charles Tuttle Leidig's birth had preceded William's by several months, so infant Willie was not the first white boy born in Yosemite.

Hutchings was in almost perpetual conflict with the Yosemite Valley Commissioners, a board of eight men appointed by the California governor to administer the Yosemite Grant. These two tracts of uniquely splendid land, encompassing Yosemite Valley and the Mariposa Grove of Big Trees, had been given to the state of California by the United States for "public use, resort and recreation."

Although the Yosemite Grant was established in 1864, the same year as Hutchings' land claim, the administration, regulation, and protection of the Grant did not begin until 1866. A guardian, respected pioneer Galen Clark, was appointed by the commissioners. After that, business concessions were regulated and a small yearly fee

William, James, and Cosie Hutchings—looking like an old lady—never lost their love for their log cabin. This picture probably was taken during James Hutchings' 1880 to 1884 term as Guardian of Yosemite. (YRL Collection)

charged for the privilege of operating within the Grant. Hutchings spearheaded the fight for private ownership through the state courts and the U.S. Supreme Court, which decided against him, and then to the state legislature, where he sought compensation.

In anticipation of greatly increased travel to Yosemite once the transcontinental railroad was opened in 1869, the commissioners granted permission for two additional hotels. Both were built in Lower Village, a mile west of Hutchings disputed domain. One, remodeled and enlarged, belonged to Alex Black, another private land claimant; the other, to Fred and Isabella Leidig.

These inns posed little competition to Hutchings, for when travel almost doubled to 1,122 in 1869, all three establishments were overcrowded. Hutchings had beds for only twenty-eight guests, Leidig's boasted fourteen "sleeping rooms," and Black's had not many more. Overflow guests slept on the floor in hallways and carpeted parlors. Improvements were "absolutely necessary," Hutchings said.

To avoid primitive and exhausting two-man pit-sawing to obtain lumber, he had machinery for a water-powered sawmill freighted in and, with difficulty, assembled. In November of 1869 he hired a "good practical sawyer" to provide the lumber needed for partitions inside his hotel, porches and lean-tos outside, and two more cottages—called River and Rock—to help accommodate the increasing visitation.

The sawyer was a thirty-one-year-old itinerant laborer, who eventually had world-wide impact but, more immediately, had beneficial influence on the sawmill and on his boss's daughters. He was Scotsman John Muir, who described Cosie as "a precious darling of a child," and, in turn, she never forgot her "small child's memories of a patient gentle man holding my sister or myself upon his knee while he showed us the composite parts of flowers . . . or of our trotting after him in the meadows looking for blossoms and their insect visitors."

"I have a mental picture," Cosie added, "of my brother when a year old sitting in a large dishpan and John Muir talking to him. That was typical of his kindly understanding for helpless things that endeared him to everyone."

Muir and his sidekick, Harry Randall, whom Hutchings had hired to milk the cow and drive the oxen, boarded with the family. Both of them enjoyed Mrs. Sproat's cooking but were skeptical of Elvira Hutchings' diet fads, and saw to it that Florence had milk from "Buttercup" when she visited the barn. Muir referred to Mrs. Sproat's muffins as "memorable," but her granddaughters preferred cornbread. "We didn't even like cornbread," Cosie admitted, "but the Indians loved it! So we swapped it to them for nupaty, a delicious little cake made from finely ground acorns, which Florence and I ate with relish."

In letters, Muir mentioned Floy as "that tameless one" and "a little black-eyed witch of a girl . . . who can scarce be overdrawn." Actually Floy, her parents, Muir, and other Valley residents were all overdrawn by Therese Yelverton, who claimed to be a countess, and who put them in a melodramatic novel, which was partly written during her prolonged 1870 visit to the Valley.

While there, she stayed in the new Rock Cottage, and became an intimate of the Hutchings family. Mrs. Yelverton's first impression of Florence appeared in her book *Zanita*.

> Her face was thin but oval, the eyes piercing black, with delicately pencilled lines, squaring a Grecian brow, broad and low with that fixed lining which gives a stare or habitual frown to her face . . . hair was dark, fine and silky.

In another chapter, Mrs. Yelverton contrasted the sisters, writing that Florence

> continued to rattle on, her imagination working and contriving, and fretting . . . whilst the little one would toddle along rejoicing in some flower, nursing it tenderly . . . exclaiming, "so pretty, so pretty!"

Before Mrs. Yelverton left Yosemite Valley for the Orient, she urged Muir to accompany her as her secretary, and asked the Hutchings if they would let her adopt Florence and train her to be an actress. Both proposals were rejected, but all of the people involved were extravagantly portrayed in *Zanita*, which featured Florence as the heroine and "Kenmuir" as the hero.

When La Casa Nevada Hotel, operated by Emily and Albert Snow, opened in 1870 on a flat near the foot of Nevada Fall, it became the custom for travelers en route to or from the high country to stop there for lunch or an overnight stay, and to sign the massive guest register. Hutchings, who often guided people to Tuolumne Meadows, was a frequent visitor, as were his daughters. On September 11, 1874, Florence, barely ten years old, made an entry that revealed a reverence not suggested by her behavior. No other fragment of her Yosemite impressions has been unearthed.

> 'Beautiful,' 'Wonderful' how come you are? for what has nature caused this awe inspiring deep canon and high towering peaks for it is to remind one there is a God, and that his works are the works of nature? that his works are wonderful beyond comprehension.

The decade of the 1870s was one of great change for the isolated chasm. The Coulterville and the Big Oak Flat stage roads to the Valley were opened in 1874, amid great celebrations. In July 1875 the Wawona Road was completed into the Valley from the south side. Hutchings figured prominently in the 1874 events but not in the one on June 22, 1875. A month earlier, after years of litigation, he had been legally evicted from his hotel, for which he had refused to pay rent to the state even after $24,000 had been awarded to him as compensation. George W. Coulter, of Coulterville, and A. J. Murphy became the new proprietors.

When he was evicted, Hutchings moved his family and office equipment into an unfinished building near Lower Village. His new "hotel" remained open until late October, when he retreated to Mrs. Sproat's San Francisco home. That had been the family's winter home ever since Floy had reached school age. Simultaneously with the upheaval, "Flora" and Gertrude Hutchings and seventeen other pupils, on July 6, 1875, began what was the regular school year to them. A log provided seating, the sky a roof. After a week or so, they met in a twelve- by sixteen foot tent, and—later still—in a former boarding house.

History of a different sort was made on October 12, 1875, at three p.m., when George Anderson stood atop 8,842-foot-high Half Dome. "All honor, then," Hutchings wrote, "to the intrepid and skillful mountaineer, George G. Anderson, who, defying and overcoming all obstacles, and at the peril of his life, became the first to plant his foot upon the exalted crown of the great Half Dome."

Next the "long, brawny, powerful Viking of a man" carried a huge coil of five-strand baling rope on his back up the steep, smooth, 975-foot climb to the top. There, Cosie Hutchings continued in her 1941 reminiscence, he "unloosed it, fastened one end to an iron pin in rock on the summit, slid it down, uncoiling and fastening it in other iron pin eye-bolts he had placed on his first ascent as he went."

Within days, a young woman and several men followed the ropeway, predecessor to today's much easier cables, and marvelled at the astonishing view. Yosemite Guardian Galen Clark, age sixty-one, was among them.

James Hutchings had left the Valley on November 1, but returned as a tourist guide the following year and climbed Half Dome twice. Florence, then thirteen, and her grandmother Sproat, sixty-five, accompanied him the second time, "daringly pulling themselves up" by Anderson's rope.

Except for such seasonal excursions the family was in exile until April 1880, when, by a political game of musical chairs, a new Board of Commissioners was appointed to supervise the Yosemite Grant—and they chose James Mason Hutchings as guardian to replace Galen Clark. Hutchings returned triumphantly to his old haunts with a new wife, Augusta, but also with his former mother-in-law Florantha Sproat and his children. It was a strange situation, since Elvira, who remained in San Francisco, kept in close touch with the children.

In 1877 John K. Barnard had succeeded Coulter and Murphy as the proprietor of the hotel complex, which consisted of Hutchings' three former cottages and a large two-story structure built by Coulter and Murphy that partly extended over the Merced River. Barnard allowed the Hutchings family to live in their "dear old cabin," and his four stepdaughters provided new friends for Floy and Cosie.

Florence displayed a dual personality. On the one hand she was bold and fearless, greeting stage passengers astride a spirited horse with a scarlet bridle. Her arresting but unladylike costume was trousers, knee-high boots, a flowing cape, and a wide-brimmed hat. When stablemen dared her to ride unruly horses she would accept the dare, and could stick on the wildest ones. She loved to gallop, would swear, and, as noted, sometimes smoked a pipe.

In contrast, she showed charm and kindness to visitors and a deep religious zeal, evidenced by her volunteer janitorial care of the Yosemite Valley Chapel, which was completed in 1879. That simple structure, which she cleaned and decorated with wildflowers, was the scene of a tragic farewell on the occasion of Effie Crippen Barnard's funeral in August of 1881. While wading in Mirror Lake, Effie had cut an artery in her foot and never recovered from the injury and loss of blood. James Hutchings conducted the service in the chapel, and Florence joined other young friends in singing "Safe in the Arms of Jesus" at Effie's grave site.

Less than a month later, on September 26, Florence died. Her funeral took place in the Big Tree Room of Barnard's Hotel, conducted by artist C. D. Robinson while her sorrowing father looked on. Floy had been critically injured when she was

Built by Hutchings as a kitchen, the Big Tree Room was used for many purposes, the saddest one being for the funeral of Florence Hutchings in 1881. The room and Cedar Cottage were torn down in 1940, but the cedar tree still stands. (YRL Collection)

unable to dodge a falling rock on the dangerous Ledge Trail, which zig-zagged almost vertically up to Glacier Point.

Long before the family was out of mourning another tragedy occurred—Augusta Hutchings died shortly after a hemorrhage of the lungs. She too was buried in the grove of oaks, and her name added to the impressive granite rock that still serves as a family headstone.

An organ was given to the Chapel in memory of Florence by an admiring woman who, Hutchings wrote, "had become devotedly attached to Floy while visiting the Valley the previous year." Surprisingly the organ's husk, but not its works, survives today.

Cosie was fourteen and William twelve when their sister and stepmother died. Two years later grandmother Sproat's death caused further emotional upheaval. Cosie was more tractable than Floy, but her individuality and her love for Yosemite were just as profound. "She was a great girl," a contemporary said, "bubbling over with life." She rode sidesaddle on a spirited horse, taking pack trips into the high country with her cousin Nellie Atkinson or close friends Alice Dudley and Laura Smith, unconcerned that "such things were not done in those days."

Eyebrows were raised when Cosie and Laura left the Valley and ran a restaurant in a mining town. They were saving money toward an uncommon goal: to attend Swarthmore College in Pennsylvania, founded in 1864 by Quakers. In 1891 Cosie arrived at Swarthmore with a dog, and for two years participated wholeheartedly in college life, but never forgot her allegiance to Yosemite.

When she arrived home again she taught school, and worked at the Wawona Hotel and at Glacier Point, where, she said, "I often built a fire of pine cones myself and pushed them over, but my firefall was skimpy." For awhile she worked in Thomas Hill's studio in the Valley, put in a stint as a telegraph operator, had something to do with a pack train, and, well after the Sierra Club was founded, was custodian of the club's Valley headquarters."

Whenever her father and his third wife came to escort tourists to the high country, there was a joyful reunion. At least once Cosie and her brother accompanied a survey party to Mt. Conness, and they probably lived together in the Valley.[1] Her marriage in 1899 and moves to other parts of the country ended her association with Yosemite for several decades, but not her interest. Both were renewed by her return there as a widow in 1941 for eight more summers in a place she had always found "so beautiful—and of dear memories."

---

1. Willy was handicapped by a spinal problem, but followed the Hutchings family tradition of cabinet making. He died, unmarried, when he was only forty.

2
Camping In Yosemite

ALICE CHASE DUDLEY was neither born nor raised in Yosemite, but she enjoyed numerous, almost yearly visits there, and her life, especially her childhood, was intimately identified with what she called "grand ole Yosemite." Her home, eight miles east of Coulterville, was an important stage stop on the pioneer Coulterville and Yosemite Turnpike Road. Before that route, advertised as "Avoiding any Horseback Riding," was completed in 1874, sites for wayside stops, where fresh teams, hay and grain, and

Alice Chase Dudley was twelve in 1879 when she accompanied friends on a month-long camping trip in Yosemite Valley. Her grandchildren and great-grandchildren still live in Mariposa County. (Mariposa Museum and History Center)

meals and lodging were available, had been chosen. Dudley's Ranch, amid pines at an elevation of 3,000 feet, was selected as the sole overnight stop between Merced and Yosemite Valley.

Even though the road hadn't been completed as far as Yosemite Valley, a surviving guest register shows that Dudley and Hubbard's opened in May 1873 and operated until late November. Two of its earliest guests were artists Thomas Hill and Albert Bierstadt. When it reopened in May 1874 it was operated by Fannie and Hosea Dudley, who continued as its hard-working and ambitious owners. From their ranch, stages covered the forty miles to the Valley in one day.

Their son, Walter Hosea, born in 1861, used his muzzle-loading shotgun to supply some of the meat served to guests. Alice, born in 1867, waited table when "Mother's help left early in the fall." Another daughter, Clara, died in 1865 at the age of six.

Thomas Edison was one of the more notable guests. Yosemite residents such as James Hutchings and Galen Clark were frequent visitors; John Muir's stops were rare. Hutchings had given his seal of approval as well as his friendship to the Dudleys, and his daughters exchanged letters and valentines with Alice and Walter. The Dudley children had been taught to keep journals by their well-educated, ex-New Englander parents. Alice's chronicle for 1879 is the basis of this account, primarily because, at the age of eleven, she became a recorder of history. When invited to accompany her Coulterville friend Katy Chadwick and Katy's parents to Yosemite Valley for a month's stay, her reaction was a delighted Yes.

Although the Chadwicks rode up "on Phil and Whitey so that Katy and I could have our horses," the girls took the stage on June 4, and "after a long pleasant ride through the forest we reached there about six o'clock," Alice wrote that night. "The Chadwick's camp, is back of Mr. Leidig's Hotel near Sentinel Creek at the base of Sentinel Rock."

Until 1906, public campgrounds were so poorly defined and so devoid of improvements or sanitation that people camped just about anywhere. Because of the Dudley connection, however, the Leidigs may have allowed, or even suggested, that the Chadwick's camp in their "backyard."

The horses had to be pastured well over a mile away. As a consequence, for the first several days the girls spent more time looking for their mounts than they did visiting the obligatory scenic spots. "Katy and I started out before breakfast this morning to find the horses, taking a few crackers in our pockets," Alice commented. "We hunted two or three hours and at last sat down to rest and eat wild strawberries." A few days later, "We caught the horses today, intending to ride up to Mirror Lake, but it was too late when we found them so we staked them near camp."

On Sunday June 8, Alice participated in a history-making event. "We went to the first Sunday School in the valley. It is a Sunday School convention." Indeed, the still unroofed, windowless, twenty-six by fifty-foot frame structure had been built partly with coins donated by children attending Sunday Schools, but the building fund was greatly augmented by contributions from prominent adult members of the Association. Their week-long convention, attracting delegates from twenty-three states, was timed to coincide with the dedication of the Yosemite Chapel. Several distinguished men had been asked to speak, and as Alice noted, "In the afternoon at 3 o'clock we went to hear the famous Mr. Vincent in front of Barnard's Hotel."

"In the afternoon of June 9," Alice added, "we went to a lecture on the geological record of Yosemite Valley by John Muir. I thought it was nice and interesting but," she admitted, "I got rather tired at the last of it and did not understand."

Two days later, "We started for Glacier Point with the Convention early in the morning. Mr. Chadwick walked all the way up, and Mrs. Chadwick, Katy and I, took turns riding Phil and Whitey.[1] We ate our lunch and then went out on the Point, and at twelve o'clock Mr. Muir began to lecture on how the valley originated, but it became so foggy that he could not show us anything so he changed the subject and told about trees. We stayed till nearly three o'clock."

That was probably the talk that persuaded a Boston orator, Dr. Joseph Cook, said to be another Daniel Webster, that Muir's glacial theories had

The Chadwick's camp was set up back of Leidig's Hotel, near the base of Sentinel Rock. (YRL Collection)

---

1. They rode and walked up the Four-Mile Trail, a toll route financed by James McCauley and built by John Conway during 1871 and 1872.

The Yosemite Valley Chapel, dedicated in June 1879 and shown here on its original site, still serves parishoners. (YRL Collection)

more validity than Professor Whitney's idea that the bottom had fallen out of the Valley.

On the following Sunday the Chadwick party attended both Sunday School and an evening prayer meeting, and again on the next Sunday. "We cleaned up to go to Sunday School today but the church was not ready so there was preaching in the public hall at 11 o'clock." Possibly work was in progress on the roof. Rafters and interior studs remained uncovered for years, and—since there was no resident pastor until 1917—services were irregular.

Alice recorded the daily routine: sightseeing by horseback to Vernal and Nevada falls one day, Bridalveil Fall another, and so on. No one walked except when looking for the horses. "We went to Glacier Point and Sentinel Dome today and had a splendid time," she wrote on June 24, and then revealed a form of amusement that now would be considered littering and destructive behavior. "We threw some bottles off Glacier Point and heard one of them strike. Katy and I threw rocks down Sentinel Dome and some of them bounded

twenty or thirty feet into the air as they rolled down. We got home about dark."

Some days the girls elected to stay around camp, playing in the river with boats that Mr. Chadwick had made for them, scrambling over the rocks, and grumbling, "for it was hot and uncomfortable." One evening, Alice wrote, "The mosquitoes are biting like fury." Fishing was almost as abortive as horse hunting. "We went fishing again today and did not get any. I would fish a while and then eat wild strawberries a while."

Mrs. Dudley relieved the tedium of camp fare by sending a box on the stage containing "bread, and rolls, apricots, and cake," Alice noted. "The fruit tasted so good."

Occasionally the girls took advantage of entertainment provided for hotel guests, probably available to them because Alice was an innkeeper's daughter. They played croquet at Black's Hotel, and one afternoon "went to Mr. Barnard's Hotel and heard Mrs. Sinning play on the piano."

Her husband, Adolph Sinning, was a skilled woodworker and ran a curio store near the hotel. On Katy's birthday, June 30, "she received a very handsome ruler. The inches are represented by twelve different kinds of wood . . . inlaid in manzanita very highly polished."

Near the end of their stay, Mrs. Chadwick, Katy, and Alice "went through the spray of Vernal Fall and up the ladder to Snow's Hotel on foot." It took money and nerve to climb up the nearly perpendicular wooden ladders through blinding spray from the waterfall. Steps had not yet been cut into the rock to create the toll-free, safer, but still wet Mist Trail we know today. "We got back to the toll house in safety, but were very wet," Alice said. "The toll house is built under the overhanging side of a boulder two or three times as big as the house." So immense was "Register Rock" that the horses could be sheltered under it.

On June 29 the girls attended Sunday School and Mrs. Chadwick a church service one last time. Two days later, the Chadwicks put Alice on the homeward-bound stage, then looked for the horses once again before riding after it. Their stay in "good ole Yosemite" was over except for the memories preserved in Alice's journal.

3

Yosemite School Days

FROM ITS INCEPTION in 1875 the Yosemite Elementary School was well stocked with the progeny of large families. During the 1870s and '80s eight Howards, seven from the Harris clan, six from the Crippen-Barnard (one mother but two fathers) family, and no fewer than ten Leidigs attended, followed by eight Kenneys and eight Degnans in the 1890s and into the 1900s. Seven Sovulewskis spanned the turn of the century and on into the 1920s. As their names suggest, a diversity of ethnic and racial backgrounds—English, Jewish, Irish, German, and Polish—was represented. Native Americans, except perhaps for the Telles family, were not as prolific, and tended to be in and out of school or were sent away to an all-Indian school.

Once a man was terminated from his job he—or, rarely, she—had to leave Yosemite along with his family, if any. For instance, when John K. Barnard was summarily fired in 1893 from his position as manager of the Sentinel Hotel, neither he nor any of his family could remain because their house had to be vacated for his successor.

There was no private enterprise in Yosemite. Leases were given to concessionaires by the Yosemite Valley Commissioners; once they were completed or broken, farewells were in order. A guardian, appointed by the commissioners, served as administrator, mayor, and judge for the establishment. Departure was often traumatic, especially for children who had no experience of cities and what was known as civilization. Larry Degnan, for example, was fourteen before he ever left Yosemite Valley. Many youngsters had never seen electric lights or a train until they left the enchanted but isolated valley. Telephones were not installed there until 1891; a water system, allowing inside plumbing in the village, in 1891 or '92; and electricity in 1903.

Only a few of the Valley's pioneers or their children left written records of their reactions or impressions of Yosemite. One was Jack Leidig who, as he aged, told bigger and more picturesque tales, but always showed pride in his pioneering parents.

When Scotland-born Isabella Dobie Leidig and her husband German-born George Frederick (Fred) Leidig rode into Yosemite Valley in May of 1866, she was nineteen, and her firstborn, George Frederick, Jr., shared her saddle. When the couple returned the following spring from wintering in Coulterville, she held baby Agnes, and the two Freds were on another horse. Fred senior was a partner in pioneer James C. Lamon's farming pursuits. In 1868 the two men planted the apple orchard that now shades a parking area at Camp Curry.

During the rigorous winter of 1868–69, the Leidigs lived in Lamon's two-story log cabin near or on the present site of the Ahwahnee Hotel. Snow was deep and food supplies were short when Agnes ate spoiled frozen peaches, and died just before Christmas of 1868. She was the first white child to be buried in Yosemite. Three months later, on March 8, 1869, Charles T. Leidig was born in the cabin where his luckless sister had died. It was an historic event: he was the first white boy to be born in Yosemite.

By that time, aided by Lamon, Fred senior was building a hotel not far from the foot of Sentinel Rock to help house the expected, and realized, influx of travelers coming to California via the transcontinental railroad. Leidig's Hotel opened on June 22, 1869, and soon the proprietress was as famous locally for her culinary skill as for her continued fecundity.

Altogether the Leidigs had eleven children—six girls and four boys who grew up in Yosemite, plus the one who died. Belle became so proficient that she delivered one infant without any assistance. Her husband was astonished when he came in from outdoor chores to find a newborn baby instead of a cup of coffee!

Large families were common, supplying a much-needed labor force for pioneering parents. Yosemite historian Jim Snyder suggests that childhood held far more drudgery than enjoyment in the nineteenth century. Still, the Leidig boys and Larry Degnan remembered their youth, on the whole, with fondness, even though their was little time to play.

Except for verbal information given by Fred junior, Charlie, and Jack Leidig as adults, and the latter's manuscript, little is known about their childhoods. Certainly Indians were integral to their lives. In the early years Fred junior had no one to play with except Indian children, from whom he picked up their language. Jack said, "Kalpine was the midwife when I was born. I helped her pick up acorns when I was a little kid."

During the pioneering years an Indian rancheria existed at the base of Sentinel Rock, back of the hotel. Some of the Indians went to Isabella for help when they had injuries; one little boy called her "Grandma" after treatment.

Jack remembered Yosemite as heaven for an outdoorsman. During the years before licenses were required, and closed seasons were unknown, he said that "Around Arch Rock at that time anybody who could fish at all could catch 50-75 nice 10 and 12 inch trout in a very short time."

One of the highlights of the '70s was ex-president U. S. Grant's visit in October of 1879. He stayed at Barnard's Hotel, but Mrs. Leidig sent her oldest sons up to see him. Even seventy-five years afterward, Jack could point out the spot where the eight-man Mariposa Band stood. His impression of the Civil War hero was less memorable: "I was very much disappointed in him. He did not look as I had expected. He looked very much like Henry Washburn." Both Henry and John Washburn, proprietors of the Wawona Hotel, were stalwart, handsome men with full beards.

Jack began school in 1881. "Seats were long benches and a small table for a desk," seating "about 16 pupils ranging in age from 7 years to 16." The rough board floor had inch-wide cracks, he noted. "Sometimes a rattlesnake would stick his head up in one of the cracks."

Jack's "recess periods were devoted to the construction of a model house from cigar boxes," an admiring Larry Degnan recorded, with Jack "whittling the pieces with a pocket knife, and nailing them together with the tiny nails or tacks from the cigar boxes."

Jack said that his father would read aloud to his brood on winter nights. "We did not have much entertainment because we always had too much work to do. Cut all of the wood by hand and

Mosquitoes, lizards, and the progeny of pioneering families attended this little, unpainted schoolhouse, which succeeded a tent, between 1877 and 1897. Mary E. Adair was the schoolmarm when this picture was taken in 1882. (YRL Collection)

Laurence was the oldest of Bridget and John Degnan's eight children. (YRL Collection)

had cows to milk and chores. In the winter we would cut wood, shovel snow and cut ice."

As a young man during the late 1890s, Jack worked for the Sentinel Hotel cutting blocks of ice out of Mirror Lake. "I had around 10 men [working] about 10 days to put up the ice for summer use at the hotel. Started when it was 5 inches thick and when the job was done sometimes it would be 10 inches." Up to 500 tons of ice were cut, and then stored in the thickly-insulated icehouse.

Long after Fred junior, Charlie, and Jack were out of grammar school, Emma, Don, Hulda, Belle, June, and Alice were enrolled. In 1888, after the Stoneman Hotel replaced "architectural bric-a-brac" such as Black's and Leidig's hotels, their builders were evicted and the buildings torn down by order of the Yosemite Valley Commissioners. Kate, the last-born Leidig, was still an infant then, and Fred junior was twenty-one.

Charlie Leidig, the first white boy born in Yosemite, was further involved in making local history. In 1898 he and Archie Leonard were appointed Special Forest Agents—in effect, park rangers. Five years later they guided and cooked for President Theodore Roosevelt and John Muir when Roosevelt visited Yosemite.

On April 2, 1889, at age five, Laurence V. Degnan began eight years of school in Yosemite Valley. His youth and his school days were the subject of his delightful reminiscences, which were published in 1956. But school was neither the most important nor unforgettable experience for young Degnan in 1889. Snow was the defining event.

Little Larry never forgot the BIG winter of 1889–90, which began, he said, with December going out like the proverbial lion. As if that weren't enough excitement, 1890 came in like "exceptionally ill-tempered lions." His childish

Kenneyville, site of Coffman and Kenney's complex of barns, shops, corrals, and employee houses, was the transportation hub of Yosemite Valley. During the years 1925 to 1927 it was replaced by The Ahwahnee Hotel. (YRL Collection)

memory of fourteen feet of snow on the level was documented, if not exceeded, by the Yosemite Valley Commissioners' biennial report for 1889–90. In addition, Degnan's father's account book recorded that he shoveled snow for three and a half days in December, fifteen and a quarter days in January, and another nine days in February. "Many of the 'days' were closer to 24 hours than to eight," Larry stated.

Bridget and John Degnan and their four small children were living in George Kenney's one-story house because "my father was acting as caretaker for a lot of barns and other buildings belonging to Coffman & Kenney, who had closed up their stable and transportation complex—now the site of the Ahwahnee Hotel—for the winter.

"All stage and other horse-drawn vehicles, saddle and harness, and other equipment and supplies were locked up in the buildings . . . [representing] a sizable lot of valuable property.

"Our house was buried in the snow, and for about a week we could not stir out. To keep the numerous buildings from collapsing under the weight of the snow, my father shoveled snow day and night from the various roofs, and had no time

to dig the family out. All he could do was shovel some snow from the roof of the house, and leave us in our snowy catacombs. Water had not yet been piped to the house, and access to the well was cut off; I remember seeing my mother stuffing snow into the kettle to melt it as an emergency water supply. Fortunately we had a covered runway to the woodshed and way stations. Later, as the emergency eased, my father dug a path to the well, and I have a vivid recollection of looking up at the towering walls of snow on each side of the path, and wondering what would become of Larry Degnan if they should topple in."

During their incarceration, Galen Clark, who had been appointed guardian for the second time the previous spring, impressed Larry because he "called on us several times on his 'Canadian' snowshoes, taking a shortcut over the buried fences of the meadow west of the house."

John Degnan had been twenty in 1883 when he married Bridget Dixon, who was three years older. Their first child, Laurence, had been "about three months old [when] my parents emigrated to the United States" from Hill of Down, Ireland. After a brief stint of ranching with already-estab-

14

lished relatives near Coulterville, they went to Yosemite Valley. Hard-workers were welcomed by Walter Dennison, the guardian at the time, and John was hired as a laborer on the roads and trails. Later, "when state work was slack," Degnan tackled "odd construction jobs for the hotels and the stage company . . . heavy manual labor during the day, mending shoes at night, and farming in his spare time." His namesake son, John Paul, credited their father with "great physical strength . . . tempered by a prudent and judicious mind that made him a loving and provident father and friend of an isolated community that often needed his services."

Like her husband, Bridget Dixon Degnan was as Irish as a shamrock, and a hard worker. Even in their first Yosemite home "in one end of an abandoned barn," Larry remembered, "my mother kept boarders, and sold an occasional loaf of bread from the Dutch oven." In retrospect, she claimed, "The first two years I was here I cried and cried." Nevertheless, behind her round-eyed colleen look, Bridget was witty, shrewd, and ambitious.

After two winters at Kenneyville, John sought and received permission from the commissioners to move into Kenney's former residence at the west end of Yosemite Village. There he began a dairy herd, and Bridget increased her production of bread. Many loaves were needed for her growing family; any excess sold for twelve and a half cents a loaf. Within a few years she bought a portable oven capable of baking fifty loaves at once. The price increased, and stabilized at twenty-five cents a loaf.

Winters were long, rigorous, and lonely for Larry. "In the winter the thirty or thirty-five permanent residents hibernated like bears, rarely stirring more than one or two hundred yards from their dens, and not seeing a new face until the stage roads were cleared (the Wawona Road, that is) for the summer mail route on April 1. Of these permanent residents the Degnan family was generally the only one with children (although once in a while Angelo Cavagnaro, who operated the store, stayed in with his family), and I had no playmate of my own sex and age. Next in age to me were my two sisters, [Mary Ellen and Daisy], who, being girls, were a total loss. Then came two

brothers, [John and Chris]—intolerable little brats, who accordingly were also a total loss; further down the line were other smaller and more incompatible nuisances, male and female [Alfred and Ruth], ending up with the ever present tiny baby [Alice]. To escape from these surroundings I tried to hang around with my father (whom I idolized on general principles) out of doors."

Winter sports were not dreamed of by pioneers, whose main vocation, winter and summer, was woodcutting, a job Larry hated. "Topping the list of chores was the never-ending task of cutting wood, and to this day I cannot think of a bucksaw without a shudder. I could tolerate an axe, and even wield it at times with enjoyment, but I cannot conceive of a more uninspiring, tedious, soul-killing piece of drudgery than crouching over a sawbuck, holding down a dry, hard, oak branch with my knee, and sawing it and hundreds like it, into stove lengths, generally with a dull bucksaw."

Occasionally, however, Larry wandered "around alone on my homemade skis, trying to find a suitable hill. In those days, instead of two small ski poles, we used a single large one, held diagonally across the body in both hands. In one particularly severe spill I landed on top of this pole, which had fallen across my path ahead of me; I thought I had broken every bone in my body."

John junior, four years younger than Larry, remembered later winter nights of fire-warmed cheer with "my father's flute and songs from the Celtic land—warrior songs and happy jigs and my mother danced around but scarcely touched the floor. Then quiet night, and family prayers and we children up to bed, where the friendly gabled window held back the storm but let in the stars."

Education was a priority for both Bridget and John Degnan, who had not had much themselves in Ireland. To augment the five- to six-month April to September Yosemite school, they employed a live-in teacher during some winters. An enrollment of five was required to keep the elementary school open, so it wasn't uncommon to enroll children as young as age five. Thus at six weeks past his fifth birthday, in April 1889, Laurence Degnan became the fifth student. The others were Kenney boys and girls. Later a few more children, notably the four youngest Leidigs, boosted enrollment.

Larry characterized his first teacher, Frances M. Hall, as excellent, "very prim and precise, but a little mite severe." He described the schoolhouse, about a third of a mile east of the Sentinel Hotel, as "a rough unpainted one-room frame shack," sixteen by twenty-four feet and with so many cracks in the walls that "friendly green lizards" and unfriendly mosquitoes easily outnumbered the students. Water had to be carried by the biggest boy from the Merced River, a hundred yards distant, and was served from a common dipper. Pine resin, used as chewing gum, was shared too, although one teacher "said that she could not chew another person's gum unless she knew that person very well!"

Maps, a globe, Webster's unabridged dictionary, slates, a blackboard, and an abacus, "which was used continually in our arithmetic lessons," composed the teaching aids. Playground equipment was non-existent, but there were large boulders to climb, and a small boggy meadow where spirited games of "prisoner's base," "one foot over the gutter," "leap frog," and "run sheep run" took place. When warm weather prevailed, swimming was the midday and after school pursuit for skinny-dipping boys. If girls insisted on joining them, the boys wore chopped-off overalls.

When Larry and other young students were wiggly and couldn't sit still, permission was given them to go outside to play or to watch Edith Jacobs, seventeen, draw an animal or a landscape. When he was older and larger, Larry graduated to water boy and, during April storms, snow shoveler, because the school roof was threatened. At least once a year, usually on a holiday, Coffman, Kenney, or John Barnard, manager of the Sentinel, would load the pupils and a couple of adults aboard one or two open carriages for a ride around the Valley.

Visitors to the school were not uncommon, and usually welcome. Once, Pike Phillips, the local character in both Yosemite Valley and Wawona, rode up outside, calling drunkenly, "I came to say good-bye; I'm goin' away tomor-hah." Flustered yet courteous, Miss Hall let two children out at a time to say goodbye, but, Larry said, Pike was riding away before "the third couple reached the porch."

Patriotism was stressed almost as strongly as the three R's—reading, 'riting, and 'rithmetic. From the morning salute to the flag and in the teacher's lectures, to the mandatory memorization of the Gettysburg Address and at least the preamble of the Constitution, the pupils were indoctrinated with the traditions and rituals of American beliefs. Much was made of both Memorial Day and the Fourth of July.

"On Memorial Day," Mary Ellen Degnan told a *Fresno Bee* reporter, "the kids from school would hike out looking for wildflowers with which to decorate the graves in our cemetery."

In contrast to the "Dead! Simply dead!" Independence Day of 1960, she claimed, "There always were flags flying, maybe a band concert, picnics and speeches . . . a community bonfire. Even the horses hauling the wagons up here used to have flags somewhere in their harness."

Away from school, Larry Degnan's education in the ways of man was furthered by firsthand observation of local politics and of what the Yosemite Valley Commissioners considered progress. By the mid 1880s Black's and Leidig's hotels were ramshackle, and the Board

McCauley's Mountain House was home to his twins, and a high-point hotel to his guests. Along with the larger Glacier Point Hotel, built in 1916, it burned to the ground in August 1969. (YRL Collection)

persuaded the state legislature to appropriate $10,000 to build what their annual report termed "an exceedingly pretty structure, of slightly Gothic suspicion, three and a half stories in height, with 80 guest rooms." Others, notably John Muir, felt that the Stoneman House was an eyesore. After it opened, in 1886, the commissioners ordered Black's and Leidig's to be demolished. Public outcry and charges of mismanagement resulted, but, boy-like, eyewitness Larry Degnan enjoyed "the terrific banging and clouds of dust . . . the screeching, ripping sound" created by the demolition.

On April 27, 1893, Larry watched the Mariposa County Sheriff serve a writ evicting John K. Barnard from his Yosemite Falls Hotel (later called the Sentinel) to Guardian Galen Clark, because Barnard was absent. Again the justice or injustice of the act escaped the boy, but he was impressed with the "tremendous heap" made by the hotel's furniture and equipment, which were dumped into the meadow near the present location of the chapel.

"Charley Kenney and I used to play with the telegraph instruments that were among the furniture, and with a mechanical race track, operated by a nickel-in-the-slot. I think we had only one nickel between us, but we could retrieve it from the unlocked receptacle into which it dropped, and run our race-horses over and over again. All the while, the high water in the meadow nibbled at the beds, and bureaus, and mattresses."

Occasionally Larry witnessed glowing embers falling in a stream from atop Glacier Point to a ledge 1,700 feet below. Although the exact origin was obscure, Larry believed that "credit for establishment of the firefall should go to James McCauley, who ran the Mountain House on the ridge back of the point. His twin sons, John and Fred, attended school by riding down their father's Four-Mile Trail mounted on burros. The trip down took ninety minutes, but the trip home took at least two and one half hours—an hour longer when the burros carried supplies for the hotel or wood for a firefall, and the boys walked.

When a visitor wanted a firefall he usually met the boys when they left school at 3:30, half an hour early as arranged with the teacher so that they would be home before dark. Degnan recalled

that the customary charge was two dollars. "The job of packing the wood and setting it up for the fire belonged to the twins, and the two-dollar fee went into their bank account." By 1897, when the family left Glacier Point, John and Fred had saved about $200 apiece, all of it hard-earned. Some of that amount came from McCauley's three-dollar charge for exploding giant powder on a special date such as the Fourth of July, or in honor of a visiting dignitary.

After McCauley's departure, Larry wrote, "The firefall and the dynamite were continued intermittently as before. I spent my college vacations working as a laborer in the valley, and on occasion I was detailed to help my father with the firefall.

"Much as I worked with dynamite, I never could overcome my fear of it, and those trips up the trail, with a sack of dynamite bouncing around behind my saddle, were never very enjoyable. On arriving at the Point, I hovered nervously around, helping my father make the bombs, tying the required number of sticks together for each bomb, crimping the treacherous copper cap on the fuse, slitting one of the outermost sticks to receive the cap, and finally, tying the whole deadly mess together for use later in the evening.

"Then we would ignite the bombs, one at a time, and lower them by a rope a hundred feet or more down the precipice, holding them in the desired position until the explosion."

It was early in the twentieth century when David A. Curry, founder of Camp Curry near the base of Glacier Point, put the firefall on a nightly basis during summers. Dynamite use was rare, however, and was eventually outlawed by the National Park Service.

McCauley's ouster from his seventeen-room, two-story hotel was another learning experience for Larry. As he recalled, "Powerful forces wanted the hotel and in the end, powerful forces took it away." At that time the commissioners, the Washburn interests, and the Southern Pacific Railroad Company were the dominant political powers.

After McCauley "had closed and boarded up the hotel for the winter" in the fall of 1897, Degnan recorded, "a gang of men, employees of the State, was sent up to the hotel from the floor of the valley, to remove McCauley's furniture and

Yosemite Valley's second schoolhouse was a recycled stage office, which served until 1917. (YRL Collection)

"My mother," Mary Ellen explained, "decided that since she was asked by so many visitors for a glass of milk, a sandwich, or something else to eat or drink, she might just as well start up a cafe or restaurant business.

"She did, too, in the dining room of our old house. Then she started a grocery store in our living room."

Larry was not thrilled, especially when his mother added ice cream to her menu. Naturally, as the eldest and huskiest of her sons, he was elected to turn the handle of the freezer.

Nor did he appreciate having to interrupt his winter vacations from school once again, "because I was the oldest, to tutor my younger brothers and sisters during the long evenings. It was just about a matter of school the year 'round."

Most of his last term in Yosemite Elementary was spent in a new frame school building about where the Le-Conte Memorial Lodge now stands. After the Stoneman House burned in August of 1896, the stage office—midway between it and the Sentinel Hotel—was abandoned, and the equipment in it moved to the Sentinel. A year later the commissioners had the office converted into a schoolhouse, one that was unattended by lizards and less frequented by mosquitoes. Cosie Hutchings was Larry's last teacher, and his "graduation" took place on November 5, 1897.

Although he enrolled again in April of 1898, he dropped out "to work as a roustabout for William Thomas, a prominent lawyer from San Francisco, who had a summer camp (with about a dozen tents and many house guests coming and going), on the very spot where Camp Curry was to start operations the following year.

"My two younger brothers had the things that I did not have, horses, guns, and the freedom to move around. My own world for most of my boyhood, was strictly limited to a small part of the floor of the valley."

Those boundaries were greatly expanded in the fall of 1898. In fact the whole year was a

other effects from the hotel—evict him by force, as it were. My father was working for the State at the time, and distasteful as the assignment was to him, he was ordered to go as a member of the gang. The hotel supplies of course, included a large quantity of choice wines and liquors, and you can imagine the condition of that gang when they arrived back in the village. It was dusk when they returned, and I was surprised to see one horse that seemed to be carrying an empty saddle. Then when the cavalcade came a little closer I could see that the rider was dead drunk and was lying flat, draped along the horn of the saddle and on the horse's neck. My father was the only sober man in the crowd, and young as I was, I felt more proud of him than if he had just been elected President."

Much as Larry loved his parents, their expectations of him were irksome. His mother's enterprise of selling homemade bread kept expanding.

pivotal one for the Degnans. As Bridget's bakery and delicatessen business had increased, so had the income and the need for bigger and better accommodations for the family and the business. John Degnan built a large two-story home with four bedrooms and two baths to house seven children, the youngest three years old. A separate bakery room, containing a wood table for kneading and a bread-rising box, was attached to the rear. Within a few years Bridget had a huge masonry and brick oven, capable of baking many loaves of bread at once. Ultimately there would be a separate building for the restaurant, ultimately the house would have additions, and, in 1902, another Degnan child, the last, would be born there.

Larry's tenure, if any, in the new house was short, because that fall, for the first time in his fourteen years, he traveled the twenty-six miles to Wawona by stage with his mother, and then boarded a train at Raymond for San Francisco.[1]

Bridget, who had not left Yosemite Valley either since 1884, was taking him to the preparatory boarding school associated with Santa Clara College (later a university)—Catholic schools that other Degnans would also attend.[2]

Laurence Degnan's observation and participation in Yosemite history continued during summer vacations. In 1905 and '06, for example, he assisted the distinguished geologist François E. Matthes in preparing a topographic map of Yosemite Valley. During two subsequent summers he worked as a draftsman for the Yosemite Valley Railroad. After retirement from a career as a civil engineer with the city of San Francisco, he began a painstaking study of Yosemite's past. Unfortunately his zeal in pursuit of documentation and his admitted procrastination in writing resulted in few published pieces, but scores of detailed letters, tinged with Irish wit, have been waiting in the Yosemite National Park Research Library for later historians.

---

1. It seems probable that Mrs. Degnan went on to San Francisco to shop for a larger bake oven. Ultimately she had an oven installed in a special room attached to the Degnan home. Built of masonry, the oven had a width of thirteen feet, a depth of thirteen feet, and a door seventeen inches high. The oven and the room are now a part of the Pioneer History Center at Wawona. One hundred loaves of bread could be baked at one time.

2. Alfred Degnan died when he was twenty, and Mary Ellen quit college in her senior year to help out at home, but Laurence, and Chris, who became a lawyer, John a physician, Ruth, and Alice all acquired university degrees.

4

Wawona Boyhood, 1884–1900

WAWONA, the 10,000-acre valley of Wawona Basin, beautifully bisected by the South Fork of the Merced River, and the Wawona Hotel complex with its 2,555-acre domain, were not part of Yosemite National Park until 1932, almost seventy years after the creation of the Yosemite Grant. That historic act, signed into law by President Abraham Lincoln in June 1864, stipulated that Yosemite Valley and the Mariposa Big Tree Grove were granted to the state of California "for public use, resort and recreation . . . inalienable for all time . . . ."

Wawona was less than six miles from the Big Trees by road, far less by trail. Therefore Wawona's development evolved around lodging, transporting, and generally servicing the awed public that wanted to see the 500 or so giant Sequoias as well as travel to the fabled valley.

The hotelkeepers, stage drivers, homesteaders, and native Indians had children who grew up in the scenic wonderland compounded of forest, meadow, river, and domes. Among them were many Bruces, and some Washburns, Gordons, and Schlageters.

Fortunately for historians, one of the ten Bruce children, a rough and ready yet perceptive boy who hated shoes, school, and rules, stored up impressions of pioneer life in Wawona that emerged decades later in his autobiography *Cougar Killer*. A few of its pages reflect a way of life and an environment rich in game that were soon diminished by homesteading and hunting.

Jay Cook Bruce was born at a mine in Mariposa County in September 1881. His father, Albert O. Bruce, then forty-two, was a master mechanic; his mother, Azelia VanCampen Bruce, age thirty, a frustrated but redoubtable woman. "Although I was the fifth child born to them," Jay related, "I was only the second one to survive." His older brother, Albert Henry Bruce, had been

born in 1879. Both were named for their father's brothers-in-law, Albert Henry Washburn and John J. Cook, who were developing the Chowchilla Mountain Road and what became the Wawona Hotel, which they had taken over from the bankrupt pioneer, Galen Clark.

One of Jay Bruce's earliest memories was of snow sifting through the cracks in a slab-sided shack onto his face and the blankets covering him and his brother Bert. Baby Harriet fared better because she slept with their mother. By then Azelia Bruce had had six children, three of whom had "passed to spirit life" in infancy, and was struggling to keep the others warm, dry, and fed on a 160-acre land claim. Her husband was working as a mechanic in a mine eighty miles away to earn the $200 due on the land, which was immediately north of the South Fork of the Merced.

Until Al Bruce filed for the land in April of 1884, he had worked for Henry Washburn as a carpenter at the Wawona Hotel. A few months later, Al was fired. Evidently Washburn, his brothers, and Cook feared that the land might be used for a competing business. The Bruces were to be starved out. By Christmas 1884 lack of meat was a real privation. Packages arrived from father Bruce and even from Aunts Jean Washburn and Fannie Cook, but as late as December 24, Jay said, his mother was "trying to think of some way to prepare canned salmon or corned beef to make these items less common." When she answered a knock on the door, it wasn't a forgiving Washburn male or one of the several middle-aged bachelors who lived within a couple of miles, but two Indians, one a barefoot boy, carrying a haunch of venison. "Tom, he shoot deer," the woman explained. "Injins think mebby you no got meat for Christmas dinner."

By the time Mary Ann and her little nephew left, they were replete with Azelia's fresh bread and coffee and a silver dollar for Tom to buy more cartridges. After that, Jay related, "The Bruce family never wanted for fresh meat the balance of the winter," nor did Tom lack money for ammunition. "Moreover, we kids had gained two redskin playmates from the 'Injin Camp.'" By then the camp had shrunk to five adults, who cared for Joe and Josey Amos—whom Jay thought to be orphans.

Subsequently "Joe always accompanied Mary Ann and played with us while his aunt was taking culinary lessons from mother." Joe was a husky lad, older and much bigger than "Bert and me put together," but even he was owl-eyed on the day he pointed out large tracks in the snow, exclaiming "Look, big lion been here purty soon. Hurry up. We better go home. Old Injin say them fellows purty bad to eat man, same as deer."

Panther jitters and winter were over before Joe showed up again and taught Bert and Jay how to make bows and arrows.

"For the next few days," Jay wrote, "arrows were kept flying and lizards 'biting the dust,' until not a reptile could be found within a radius of five hundred feet around our dwelling. We continued to improve our models and use them for practicing on all kinds of small pests, including ground squirrels."

When the brothers wanted to emulate their barefoot tutor, Jay said, "mother objected, saying

a snake might bite us. Jay retorted thus: 'Them snakes, he don't chase man. Anyhow we run like deer without shoes on.'"

By July 1886, the family hiatus was resolved, Al Bruce had been rehired at the hotel, and the Bruces' newest child, named for Aunt Jean Bruce Washburn, was born. On weekends and after dinner, Al cleared, plowed, and planted on his acreage, aided by his wife and sons. In time, he built an attractive and substantial two-story house with a gable over the front porch. Hard times were alleviated, but not over.

Possibly the worst time was described by daughter Harriet to the author in 1960.

In "the winter of 1888–89 the snow piled six feet on the level, the hay gave out in the barn and it took from four o'clock in the morning till ten at night to get the team to a Washburn barn" less than two miles away.

Three more sons—Edward, named for Edward Washburn, William, and Robert—were born by 1895, making even more appetites to satisfy. Al Bruce taught the two oldest, Bert and Jay, to load and shoot his muzzleloader. As a result, by 1891, when Bert was twelve and Jay ten, "We had found a way to earn a few dollars, while providing meat for our table." In his book, Jay explained ingenuously, or perhaps defensively, "At the same time we were protecting the source of that meat supply from the depredations by the predators taken incidentally. For those half dozen animals—foxes and wildcats combined— we killed that winter would necessarily have had to kill three hundred squirrels each year they lived—six times the number we used."

After landscape artist Thomas Hill's daughter Estella married John Washburn, Hill worked in a studio near the main Wawona Hotel building. His fine paintings, affable

Wawona Hotel, about 1886. (Wawona Washburn Hartwig Collection)

personality, and picturesque studio intrigued guests. Animal skins, Indian baskets, wasps' nests, and other curios festooned the walls, and trout swam in the fountain outside. Many tourists bought paintings from him; others purchased such curiosities as rattlesnake skins and rattles. Hill paid the Bruce brothers for them as well as for animal pelts they had shot and tanned. Squirrel pelts were worth fifty cents apiece. Jay wrote: "It looked like we wouldn't have to ask dad for money to buy powder and caps for our 'shootin' irons. There was something else we wanted too— a harmonica apiece, things which had to be purchased in Raymond, and could be gotten through the courtesy of any stage driver."

Nathaniel "Pike" Phillips showed them how to splice together rattlesnake "buttons" from several snakes to make impressive strings to sell to credulous tourists. Jay tried Pike's method "until mother got wise and forbade us to cheat. We managed to sneak away and find a rattlesnake often enough to keep us supplied with money to purchase powder and caps."

Even though Bert, Jay, and the younger Bruces had home teaching from their mother, who had taught school before her marriage, they had never attended a real all-day school until May of 1892, when the Wawona Grammar School opened. The three R's were dispensed by Cosie Hutchings in one room of the stage drivers boarding house. As if that weren't diverting enough, pets belonging to her sixteen students, and peacocks from the hotel, were in and out. "For instance," Cosie recounted long afterwards, "a small dog— 'Whiskers' by name—was a regular attendant," as was the Leonard girls' brown setter Flora. She produced a litter underneath the room's floor that "caused a great deal of excitement, since she refused to allow the puppies to venture forth into the eager hands of the school children until they were able to look out for themselves."

Several Bruces, the Leonard girls—who were half Indian—and Joe were among the disparate student body. Jay and Bert, at eleven and thirteen respectively, were unhappy with the restrictions inherent in a school whose term coincided with spring, summer, and fall—the best seasons to fish, hunt, and roam. Sometimes they resorted to playing hookey.

In 1894, while enjoying a tumultuous Fourth of July holiday, Jay "was carelessly celebrating with some homemade bombs, foolishly picking up one that I thought was not going to explode. It did— blasting my hands and face with fragments of copper. Although my father did his best to extract the pieces, many remained embedded. Two weeks after the accident, my wounds were healed but my fingers were stiff and both hands very tender. Father hired an Indian to cut up enough stove wood to last us for a month. I could have gone to school, but I had another idea in mind—going fishing. I persuaded mother that I couldn't possibly hold a book or pencil for some time to come, although I did manage to hold a willow pole and cast with it."

Jay applied himself, as he never did in school, to concentrated study of what lured trout, why, and when. He discovered that they were "wary of anything that looks unnatural, such as a white shirt or glistening straw hat." Thereafter he wore "clothes that blend with the foliage on stream banks." He used a reel-less willow fishing pole, and mutilated flies—made of chicken feathers— with his teeth so that they would "look good to the fish." By these unorthodox methods he increased his afternoon catches from five or ten fish to as many as fifty.

At first, fresh fish were an "uncommon luxury" to the Bruces, who rarely paid the twenty-five cents a pound charged by an Indian, but before long trout "had become 'a drug on the market' at our house," Jay admitted. Happily for him, campers paid him enough so that he could afford "a multiplying reel line," which he painted brown so that the nickel-plated reel wouldn't alert fish to his casts.

In September the reluctant scholar was offered another "disagreeable" task besides fishing. "The venerable Thomas Hill decided he wanted to eat two or three mountain quail each week and picked on me to supply them. He provided me with a single-shot, 22-caliber rifle and five hundred bb caps with which to do the hunting. Now I was in my glory, with a good trout rod and a rifle with plenty of ammunition on hand and no wood to chop. I even thanked my lucky stars for that bomb exploding in my hands and maiming them to such an extent that I couldn't be expected to swing an ax. Instead of riding to school I hiked through the forests, sniping quail, doves and squirrels. The latter two creatures, not suiting the taste of the famous artist, always went into the Bruce family pot to be stewed with dumplings. When Mr. Hill left Wawona in November to spend the winter at Coronado in San Diego County, he presented the rifle and remaining cartridges to me."

Not even that gun completely satisfied the young hunter, but two more gifts—a 44-caliber 1873 model Winchester rifle and a 16-gauge muzzleloading shotgun—did. "Using these two weapons I kept our table well supplied with wild meat—chiefly squirrel, quail and grouse—for the next several years." Deer weren't safe from Jay either, and, in time, he bagged bears, but not the feared grizzly. Jim Duncan was the famed bear hunter of the time, accounting for eighty to ninety bears, including grizzlies, mainly in the Wawona Basin. Homesteaders were not abnormally bloodthirsty, but deer ate crops, bear ate livestock, and consequently Duncan provided fresh game for hotel guests.

By 1896, the year Jay turned fifteen, he was judged old enough and big enough (120 pounds and five feet ten inches) to go to work to help support nine Bruces. By then the Wawona Hotel had five buildings to house guests, and was amazingly self-sustaining. Vegetables, apples, potatoes, chickens, hogs, cattle, and a dairy assured diners of nutritious and delicious meals.

The Washburn brothers even had a fish hatchery built on their land to keep the South Fork well-stocked. They had their own sawmill, blacksmith and carpentry shops, a slaughter house, a water system, and an ice pond that doubled as a lake in summers. They employed a large work force, and Jay was hired not because of nepotism but for his proven abilities.

"My first few jobs," he remembered, "were typical of the period and the people—pick and shovel laborer on the road gang, farm hand, fire fighter, stage driver, farm hand again. The jobs were temporary—geared to the work that had to be done and the season of the year.

"In the spring of 1899 my ability to catch trout began really to pay off in cash and at the same time freed me from the farm job I hated. I had been milking twenty-five cows and doing the ranch chores, a job which kept me busy ten hours per day, seven days a week, without getting any pay at all for Sunday work. Mr. Washburn, at the hotel, lost his Indian supply of trout and commissioned me to catch them for the hotel diners."

During the spring and summer of 1899 and 1900, Jay said, he "whipped the trout streams (principally the South Fork) four to eight hours a day and caught some 32,000 trout." A bit defensively, he added that just twenty-one pairs of rainbow trout could reproduce "the 16,000 I took annually," since "an average two-year-old female spawns about 750 eggs a season." Bruce's successor as the hotel fish supplier may have been Clarence Washburn, son of John Washburn and nephew of the other two brothers. On one college vacation, his biggest catch was 297 trout in a single day.

Jay's career as a fisherman ended with the turn of the century because, he stated, of "a law prohibiting the sale of trout." Eventually, utilizing his Wawona-learned skills as a hunter, Jay went to work for the State Fish and Game Commission and became their chief lion hunter. His autobiography, *Cougar Killer*, published in 1953, chronicled his and the state's unwise near-decimation of mountain lions. After 1932, when the Wawona Basin and Washburn property became part of Yosemite National Park, hunting was prohibited. Although wildlife in the area has never regained its former prolific diversity, mountain lions are still among the population.

5

Childhood of Enchantment, 1894–1910

Bᴇᴄᴀᴜsᴇ "No one had consulted me ahead of time," Marjorie Cook Wilson reminisced, "I was born in San Francisco. Had I been asked, I would have chosen Yosemite Valley regardless of the fact there was no hospital, no doctor and no nurse there till many years after my arrival." Several months after her birth, late in 1893, infant Marjorie, her mother, May C. Cook, and a Scottish nurse arrived in an open, snow-blanketed buckboard at the Sentinel Hotel, where her anxious young father, Jay Bruce Cook, welcomed them.

Cook was the son of John Jay Cook, a pioneer entrepreneur often associated with the Washburn interests. His mother, Fannie, was Albert Bruce's sister—and thus an aunt to his eight children—and Henry Washburn's sister-in-law. Cook, who was twenty-six years old in 1894, had assisted his father in the management of the eighty-room, three-and-a-half story Stoneman House after it

Early in 1894 infant Marjorie Cook arrived at the Sentinel Hotel in an open buckboard.
The hotel was to be her beloved home for her entire childhood. (YRL Collection)

In profile, the main building of the six-cottage Sentinel Hotel resembled a riverboat. Guests could fish from the porch. (YRL Collection)

Ivy Cottage and the twenty-four-room Oak Cottage to accommodate the increased demand for rooms caused by the loss of the Stoneman House. Altogether the complex consisted of eighty-six rooms, and after the senior Cook's death in 1904 his son, Jay, was the sole proprietor.

Until the advent of Camp Curry, in 1899, the Sentinel offered the only remaining accommodations in Yosemite Valley. In the "June rush, that meant two in every bed, children on folding cots and a squeeze all around," Marjorie commented. Besides the main hotel building, widely-scattered cottages "accommodated sixty more guests. Each cottage took its name from its surroundings. Wobbly old Locust Cottage, sitting in a grove of slender locust trees, was only used when every other place was filled to bursting. River Cottage did not actually overhang the river as the adjoining main building did but it was close enough to hear the water singing. The upstairs bedrooms had floor to ceiling French doors. I thought them very elegant but tourists did not share my feelings. When they opened a door to get light and air, they practically dressed on the porch.

"Across the road, Rock Cottage sat in a pile of boulders, the largest nearly as big as the building itself." In 1897 Cook had directed the remodeling of the already venerable Cedar Cottage so that bedrooms were created downstairs. In addition, flooring was installed around the cedar tree in the Big Tree Room. However, Marjorie reported that the fireplace built by Hutchings smoked, and every [rain] shower leaked in between the tree and the roof. We overcame the leak by planting five-finger ferns which did very well at the base of the tree." Guests used the room as a lounge, and ladies shrieked when a snake poked its head above the ferns.

"A wash stand, a bowl, pitcher of cold water and a supply of clean towels stood in each room. Hot water was brought from the kitchen upon

opened, in 1888. During winters, when it was closed, young Cook assisted Albert Glasscock, proprietor of the ex-Hutchings, ex-Coulter and Murphy, ex-Barnard's Hotel, newly christened the Sentinel Hotel.

"My Semty Valley," Marjorie recounted many years later in an unpublished manuscript, was home "for eighteen carefree years . . . a childhood of enchantment." After the Stoneman House was destroyed by fire, in 1896, and after Glasscock's death the following year, her father, Jay B. Cook, managed the Sentinel complex of four old-fashioned guest units. He added the eight-room request. Separate buildings housed the plumbing. When Half Dome blushed all rosy in sunset, few people could remember they did not have a private bath."

Until 1906 the Yosemite Grant, consisting of Yosemite Valley and the Mariposa Grove, continued to be governed by a succession of guardians—some good, others inept—and seven commissioners. All of them were appointed by whoever was governor of California. Inevitably most were fat cats, being rewarded by the governor for political favors. Marjorie's opinion of them, doubtless mirroring that of her father, was poor. "I liked June with its varying excitement. Those who worked in the valley found it a most difficult month. After every crack and corner had been reserved for paying guests who were entitled to first consideration, the commissioners and their friends descended upon us unannounced. The majority were dead heads and most of them felt they rated special attention. They managed to make themselves quite a problem."

For years the Cook family lived over the

kitchen, and were consequently quite warm if not actually overheated. "The room shook with the pressure of spring freshets against the old foundation. We finally moved to the newest of all the scattered buildings, Ivy Cottage, between Locust and River cottages. There we had a private bath, a fireplace and a summer sitting room on the porch."

From infancy, Marjorie had firm friends among the Sentinel's staff. "Our various Chinese, like the Indians, regretted I was not a boy, but were more than kind and tolerant to the small girl-child. Each spring, I eagerly awaited my meeting with the Ah clan. At an early age, I gratefully accepted a fragile, twenty-two piece green and gold (Chinese) tea set. I loved every dragon. The next spring, the head man, Ah Wong, brought a gorgeous Chinese fan nearly half as tall as I."

Ah Wong, Ah Mow, Ah Toy, and several other Chinese returned yearly for the customary April 1 opening of the hotel. At that time of year the kitchen and a long section of the porch overhung the Merced River. Sometimes, Marjorie said,

Rock Cottage was built in 1870 by James Hutchings amid granite boulders.
One, Marjorie said, was "nearly as big as the building itself." (YRL Collection)

"Fishermen found it most convenient to set their lines and sit down to lunch or dinner on the porch. Many a meal was interrupted while someone landed a nice big trout—our Chinese cooks were always willing to transfer the fish from hook to skillet."

The Chinese staff preferred living together in a crowded bunkhouse, and wanted their pay in currency. Ah Toy stored his hoard of bills in a paper bag under his mattress. "One day," Marjorie recounted, "he came to Mother almost in tears and held out a big handful of well chewed green paper.

"'Mouses making nest in my bed. This my moneys. You fix, please.'

"Dad boxed up the mess, just as it was, and sent it to the San Francisco mint with a letter telling how it had happened and the amount he thought the nest was worth. After some delay, Ah Toy received most of his money back with a scolding letter and a can of rodent exterminator."

Ah Toy asked Mrs. Cook to teach him English, "and they both worked hard. When he spelled, 'E two times gee,' and looked hopeful, Mother tried to give him a hint, 'You know, Toy, something you cook every morning.' 'Oh yes, hotcakes!' was his triumphal reply."

Like the Chinese, local Indians pitied Jay Cook, because, Marjorie explained, "I was not a boy but I was always content to be their waino muchacha (good girl). I recall our later contacts with pleasure and pity. They had so little; they had been deprived of so much. They were old, tired, beaten, and distrustful of most whites. Lancisco would not enter any white man's house but he did pad silently, in his moccasins made from old barley sacks, to the front of the back stairs until Dad carried me out. He looked, grunted and went his lonely way."

Marjorie admired Lancisco because "He never begged and seldom accepted handouts. That meant he was pitifully thin and dressed in rags. Day after day, he fished along the bank of the river with a willow pole and angle worms for bait. The few trout he caught, he sold to the hotel. As soon as I could read the scales, the duty of weighing Lancisco's fish became mine and no butcher ever weighed a heavier thumb. Even then, it was a mere pittance he received each night."

Marjorie devoted more than three chapters of her manuscript to Native Americans, their legends, and their adaptation to a debased way of life. She wrote that "Old Mary called often, entered without knocking and sometimes brought her friends to cast envious eyes at Mother's fine collection of Indian baskets and bead work. Now and then she related Indian gossip for miles around. She also added commentaries on passing tourists. I have known her to sit for the better part of an hour, looking perfectly dumb and murmuring, 'Me no savvy.' When a well-intentioned but condescending tourist left, Mary would chuckle deep inside her ample tummy and tell us, in pidgin English, what she thought about everything from the lady's shoes to her hat. That included manners and morals and Mary was pretty sure to be right in what she said."

At the fall fandangos, Marjorie claimed, "Francisco was by far the best dancer. His nearly naked body, carefully oiled and wet with sweat, glistened like polished copper; his movements were as smooth as a running deer and there was no tiring him. He chanted most of the time he danced. Each year, I begged to stay as long as Francisco danced but when I left (under protest) he seemed as fresh as he had been hours before. I never saw the end of a fandango.

"At these fandangos, the Indians served jerked deer and bear meat, smoked fish, acorn mush and bread and many other dishes less easy to identify. I had never even heard of a germ and I liked Indian food so I got along without any discomfort. Once, when Mother took a friend with us, the city-bred lady had a hard time and I did not help much by telling her the unknown paste might be beaten grasshoppers or grubs."

Sally Ann Dick was often disdained because of her reaction to the white man's liquor, but Marjorie defended her. "Blind Dick lived longer than any other Ahwahneechee warrior. Perhaps because his daughter, Sally Ann, cared for him whenever she thought about it. Sally Ann was erratic and sometimes she drank but she was good to her feeble old father. They had a decent cabin and Sally Ann worked in the hotel laundry or, now and then, as nurse for the child of some mountain climbing tourist."

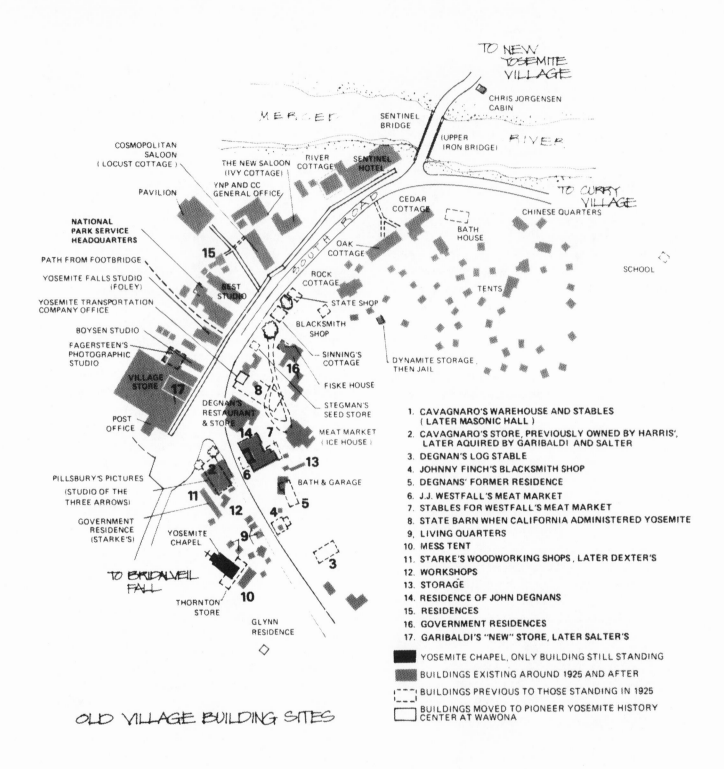

TO NEW YOSEMITE VILLAGE

CHRIS JORGENSEN CABIN

MERCED RIVER

SENTINEL BRIDGE

(UPPER IRON BRIDGE)

TO CURRY VILLAGE

COSMOPOLITAN SALOON (LOCUST COTTAGE)

THE NEW SALOON (IVY COTTAGE)

RIVER COTTAGE

SENTINEL HOTEL

PAVILION

YNP AND CC GENERAL OFFICE

CEDAR COTTAGE

CHINESE QUARTERS

BATH HOUSE

NATIONAL PARK SERVICE HEADQUARTERS

15

SOUTH ROAD

OAK COTTAGE

SCHOOL

PATH FROM FOOTBRIDGE

ROCK COTTAGE

TENTS

YOSEMITE FALLS STUDIO (FOLEY)

BEST STUDIO

YOSEMITE TRANSPORTATION COMPANY OFFICE

STATE SHOP

BOYSEN STUDIO

BLACKSMITH SHOP

FAGERSTEEN'S PHOTOGRAPHIC STUDIO

16

SINNING'S COTTAGE

DYNAMITE STORAGE, THEN JAIL.

VILLAGE STORE

17

8

FISKE HOUSE

POST OFFICE

DEGNAN'S RESTAURANT & STORE

14

7

STEGMAN'S SEED STORE

MEAT MARKET (ICE HOUSE)

13

2

BATH & GARAGE

6

PILLSBURY'S PICTURES (STUDIO OF THE THREE ARROWS)

11

12

4

5

GOVERNMENT RESIDENCE (STARKE'S)

9

YOSEMITE CHAPEL

3

TO BRIDALVEIL FALL

THORNTON STORE

10

GLYNN RESIDENCE

1. CAVAGNARO'S WAREHOUSE AND STABLES (LATER MASONIC HALL)
2. CAVAGNARO'S STORE, PREVIOUSLY OWNED BY HARRIS', LATER AQUIRED BY GARIBALDI AND SALTER
3. DEGNAN'S LOG STABLE
4. JOHNNY FINCH'S BLACKSMITH SHOP
5. DEGNANS' FORMER RESIDENCE
6. J.J. WESTFALL'S MEAT MARKET
7. STABLES FOR WESTFALL'S MEAT MARKET
8. STATE BARN WHEN CALIFORNIA ADMINISTERED YOSEMITE
9. LIVING QUARTERS
10. MESS TENT
11. STARKE'S WOODWORKING SHOPS, LATER DEXTER'S
12. WORKSHOPS
13. STORAGE
14. RESIDENCE OF JOHN DEGNANS
15. RESIDENCES
16. GOVERNMENT RESIDENCES
17. GARIBALDI'S "NEW" STORE, LATER SALTER'S

■ YOSEMITE CHAPEL, ONLY BUILDING STILL STANDING

▨ BUILDINGS EXISTING AROUND 1925 AND AFTER

⌐⌐⌐ BUILDINGS PREVIOUS TO THOSE STANDING IN 1925

☐ BUILDINGS MOVED TO PIONEER YOSEMITE HISTORY CENTER AT WAWONA

OLD VILLAGE BUILDING SITES

In its heyday, Yosemite Village stretched from Sentinel Bridge to the still-standing Yosemite Valley Chapel. (*Historic Resource Study,* Linda W. Greene, vol. 3, 1987)

Marjorie and her mother and father invariably befriended the Native Americans, whether local or from a visiting tribe. They "seldom said thank you in words," was Marjorie's comment. "They did nice things," such as giving away beaded or woven work that they had painstakingly made.

Much as she admired the Indians, Marjorie was grateful that she had escaped being christened Tissiac, Loiya, Wawona, Yosemite, Pohono or, worst of all, Illilouette, names "a June visitor (or even a local resident) [might] choose to commemorate their stay in Yosemite. Boys were never honored in that way."

Marjorie herself was honored when Sally Ann Dick Castagnetto named her only daughter Marjorie.

Jay Cook leased more than an acre of land as a garden plot, where he grew vegetables needed for the dining room, along with flowers planted under his wife's supervision. All summer, "roses furnished table decorations," Marjorie recalled proudly, "and giant pansies adorned the parlor table. Our sweet peas grew so tall Mother had to have help to gather them.

"Every now and then, Mother and I took the buggy and went after wild flowers. We picked

Marjorie was spoiled by her father, "Uncle Harry" Washburn, the Chinese help, and the Indians, but not by her mother, who was loving yet firm. (YRL Collection)

with shears; left plenty for seed and never hurt a bush or pulled a bulb. At Happy Isles, we found woodwardia ferns higher than my head. The best dogwood grew near Pohono Bridge. We gathered that in spring for its pure white blooms, in fall for the flaming foliage. Bleeding heart and columbine grew near Pohono Bridge too. Small flowers like cyclamen, nemophilia or mist maidens took an awful lot of picking in the hot sun.

"In reality, the entire floor of the valley was our garden. We often pruned, sometimes weeded and occasionally watered a long way from home."

Mrs. Cook was loving, but at times a disciplinarian. "On those occasions when I was sent to bed with only a large bowl of bread and milk between me and starvation," Marjorie commented, "housekeeper Lizzie Murphy, waitress Kittie Tatch and proprietor Jay Bruce Cook combined to see that plenty of dessert was added to my menu." It was long afterward before Marjorie realized that her understanding mother had known of the connivance.

Ever since 1879 the Yosemite Chapel had been the scene of weddings, an occasional funeral, and the irregular Sunday services conducted by vacationing ministers. By 1901 the chapel was isolated from community activities, because the only buildings left in Lower Village were the homes of George Fiske and Galen Clark. Consequently, Marjorie said, "the Chapel was taken apart and moved to the spot where the village and the meadow met [where it still stands] and the yellow evening primroses grew close to the door."

Before the pews were reinstalled a visiting minister agreed to conduct a service. Carpenters hurriedly nailed supports to the floor and laid boards across them. Marjorie and Dorothy Atkinson sat in the front row, but Mrs. Cook was on a bench in the back close to the wall. No one else was near her until "Mrs. [Angela Ghirardelli] Jorgensen rushed in late and sat hard on the aisle end. She weighed nearly twice what Mother did. Mother flew up in the air and gave a stifled scream. As she bounced, she seized the hat of the lady directly in front of her." Pandemonium ensued.

On more normal Sundays, Marjorie admitted that her "religion depended entirely on who happened to be conducting services. One week

I was a Methodist, the next a Catholic or maybe a Seventh Day Adventist."

In contrast to his wife, artist Chris Jorgensen was a small man; and, Marjorie felt, a bombastic one. For three summers he camped on the river bank northeast of and across the Merced from the Sentinel Hotel.

In 1900 he obtained a concession from the Yosemite Valley Commissioners to build a combination studio and home on the same site. "Old timers tried to tell him he would be in the middle of the river at the first high water but he built his home exactly where he wanted it to be," Marjorie recorded. A year or so later, "At the beginning of a freshet, the [four] Jorgensens strolled over to the hotel for dinner. At eight o'clock they were warned the river was rising and they better leave. Mrs. Jorgensen laughed. Mr. Jorgensen swore and they stayed where they were until ten thirty. Then Mr. Jorgensen lighted his lantern and guided his family across the bridge. That was as far as they got for what had been a meadow at sunset, was part of a broad river and the [two-story] house looked like Noah's Ark.

"Mr. Jorgensen waded in icy water above his waist before he reached his front door. He packed what the family needed and meekly came back to the hotel for the night." Fortunately the house was elevated enough so that the rooms, and his fine paintings, were not harmed. Afterward, he had a foot bridge built from the road to his porch, and expensive rock work done on the river's bank.

Marjorie's best friend was Dorothy Atkinson, and her second home was that of the Atkinsons, across the road from the Sentinel Hotel. Dorothy's father, Charles Atkinson, was a jack-of-many-trades who worked for the Yosemite Valley Commissioners. His wife, pretty Nellie Atkinson, was also versatile.

Before her marriage, in 1892, Nellie had waited tables at the Stoneman House, retouched and sold photographs for George Fiske, learned from Indian women how to do skilled beadwork, and became an expert on their basketry. Whatever Nellie did she did with a wholehearted love of life that delighted her three children as well as Marjorie Cook. Dorothy was only nine months older than Marjorie; Ned and Little Bill were younger. Nellie took them on picnics that Mar-

jorie recalled as a combination "bird walk, nature study tour, flower hunt," and they returned to the Village with bouquets, and berries for cobblers, jams, and jellies.

Little Bill's death of typhoid at age three was the first tragedy the children encountered. After that, Marjorie said, "We visited the cemetery often and stayed long enough to coax extra water from the squeaky cemetery pump to care for the garden around Mr. Clark's empty grave." Thirty years before ex-guardian Galen Clark's death at age ninety-six, he had begun to prepare his own gravesite. Not only had he selected "a fine slab of granite for a tombstone," but had enclosed the hole he dug with a white fence, and soon had "hardy red roses" climbing over the rails.

Marjorie admired him as a "gentle old man" who taught her that "There is nothing so lovely as LOVE and nothing so hateful as hate." On April 2, 1910, Jay Cook was a pallbearer at Clark's funeral, and Marjorie and other school children dropped wreaths of pine and blossoms atop the casket of Yosemite's pioneer before he was lowered into the space he had prepared.

In 1902, Marjorie, Dorothy, and Ned were infuriated when electricity came to Yosemite Valley. "We were willing to accept inside lights; outdoors we definitely preferred the moon. They built the dynamo below Happy Isles and all the way down to the village, placed poles at short intervals. Each pole supported a string of wires and an ugly arc light. Before the actual pole appeared, workmen drove stakes where it was to be. We three pulled up every stake and threw it in the river. We objected violently to the big branches they cut from some of the beautiful trees. They trimmed to suit the wires and paid no attention to the misshapen tree they left."

A fringe benefit was Charlie Atkinson's steady employment to operate the power plant for the Yosemite Valley Commissioners. "In winter," Marjorie recorded, "he blinked the lights at nine forty five as a signal you had fifteen minutes to get to bed if you wanted to do it by electric light."

During summers Charlie worked nights, a nuisance, Marjorie felt, since "in order to let Mr. Atkinson sleep, we had to almost stop using our play house in the Atkinson attic."

Most well-known guests, such as novelist

Galen Clark's funeral. The children, left to right: Harlow Parks, Lillian Parks, Alice Degnan, Mildred Sovulewski, Eugene Tucker, Evelyn Tucker, Ellen Boysen, and Grace Sovulewski. In back: George Fiske and John Degnan. (YRL Collection)

Gertrude Atherton, turned out to be so ordinary that the children were unimpressed. But in May of 1903 they were thrilled when they heard that President Theodore Roosevelt, the famous Rough Rider hero of the Spanish-American War, was coming. Marjorie was privy to the elaborate preparations at the Sentinel Hotel. "From San Francisco," she wrote, "came a contingent of great, near great and would-be great. The commissioners arrived in a body feeling duly important. The chef from San Francisco's famous Bohemian Club not only came to take charge of the banquet, he brought a large amount of food with him.

"Reports from the presidential party, happily encamped in some high mountain meadow, varied from day to day. On one thing they [Roosevelt and John Muir] were most definite. This was a vacation and there would be no banquet. As we waited, the Bohemian Club food spoiled and the Bohemian Club chef left in a rage. That delighted our Ah Mow, who had found him an intolerable nuisance.

"Schools as far away as Coulterville closed and teachers, pupils and their families hitched their best horses to their best conveyances and drove

miles to Yosemite where they camped while they waited. The owner of the local store declared he did not care if the president never showed up as long as he kept people interested and hungry.

"In the meantime, the president, accompanied by John Muir, Archie Leonard and Charlie Leidig continued to stay out of sight. Muir had been selected for his scientific knowledge and his deep love of the mountains. Archie Leonard was one of the best guides. He also knew how to pack a mule properly. Besides being the first white boy born in the valley, Charlie Leidig was a mighty good camp cook. The official presidential party, including the secret service men, was left at Wawona.

"When the big day did arrive, the commissioners, convinced they could not make speeches at a banquet, took a picnic lunch and hid out till the excitement was over. No one missed them.

"Dorothy and I spent the entire morning out in the hot sun gathering white violets to present to the president. We were also set to make a speech we had written and memorized for the occasion. It was to be delivered, with appropriate gestures, as a great surprise to every one including our parents. It is probably fortunate it was never made.

31

President Theodore Roosevelt's visit in May 1903 occasioned great excitement among hero-worshiping children and adults. His companion, John Muir, was secondary. (YRL Collection)

"Finally, the hour set for the presidential entrance came. We hung over the railing of the upper porch and clutched our fast fading violets as we stared up the road. After what seemed like a lifetime of waiting, a cloud of dust appeared and we raced each other down stairs to spread the news.

"I do not know what we expected to ride out of that dust cloud. Certainly not a camp-soiled man in khaki pants and a torn sweater. Before we recovered from the shock, the president had acknowledged the cheers of the waiting people, ridden under that ungraceful welcome sign without seeing it and disappeared in the Jorgensen studio. We hurried across the bridge and established ourselves, one on each side of the entrance to the studio grounds and before even we had a chance to become impatient, the presidential party emerged again. As he approached, we crowded close, stuck out the violets and opened our mouths to begin our speech. He saw us, gave that famous grin, shook our outstretched hands crushing the violets completely, said, "Hello, little girls," and was gone.

"We forgot the speech, we forgot the violets which we still held. We only knew that the Rough Rider, Teddy Roosevelt, our beloved hero and President, had actually shaken hands and spoken to us. We dashed across the bridge directly behind the president's horse only to see our lovely balloon of importance blow up in our faces when a boy who did not even live in the valley got more attention than we had received.

"As they trotted past the hotel down the carefully sprinkled road, a strange boy perched atop our garden fence called, 'Hello, Teddy.' The president rode over to the fence and read the unknown a good sound lecture on the subject of the respect due the president. The boy looked scared, gasped, 'Yes, Sir, Mr. President,' and climbed off the fence.

"Never did a scolding go so completely astray. That boy was the envy of all the children and most of the grownups too. Our hasty hand shake and three word greeting paled into insignificance, [but] the president was still our hero.

"Mr. Roosevelt and the three men with him [Muir, Leonard, and Leidig] camped in the Bridal Veil Meadows that night.[1] There were no fireworks, no one had a chance to make a speech. Most of the visitors went home somewhat disgusted, but two hero worshipping little girls and one rather embarrassed little boy were well content."

School days still prevailed all summer, but Marjorie remembered that "One winter, two extra families stayed and, counting me, it made just enough to keep the school open. I had never been

---

1. While Charlie Leidig shooed people away that evening, Muir and Roosevelt talked about the need for forest protection. Later in his administration, Roosevelt created five national parks, twenty-three national monuments, and 143 national forests.

to school and at first, I thought it was a great treat." She could read fluently, but her knowledge of arithmetic was so faulty that the teacher worked to improve it the entire term, and "offered to coach me after hours, The other children were not grateful to me for spoiling their winter vacation. By spring I did not blame them."

Jay Cook was responsible for an exciting diversion when he loaded pupils and teacher into his sleigh for a ride. Sleigh rides "on sunny days and moonlight nights, ice skating, skiing and frosty toes" were winter activities. "In the evenings, there were taffy pulls with prizes for the whitest candy and Dorothy and I were forever acquiring blisters because we started to pull when it was too hot."

Marjorie's affections extended to Wawona and its New England-style Wawona Hotel, because Ah You, its head chef, always gave her a sugar cookie "even when I grew so tall I was ashamed to accept" it. Her beloved "Uncle Harry," (Albert Henry Washburn, actually her father's uncle), was the oldest, most prominent, and most powerful of the three Washburn brothers. He was the outside man, in charge of transportation and promotion. As superintendent of the monopolistic Yosemite Stage & Turnpike Company he was on the road a great deal, and Marjorie "waited eagerly for his frequent visits to My Semty Valley."

Rides on his shoulders as he toured the Company's "big, hot, odoriferous barns," chewing horehound or peppermint sticks, were thrills to a small girl. "Uncle Harry knew all the hostlers and drivers and most of the horses by name," Marjorie remembered. It was he who, without her mother's knowledge, supervised Marjorie's first haircut, he who took her on her initial tour through the Mariposa Grove of Big Trees and cradled her head when she wept from sheer awe.

"One fall, Dad was asked to stay over at Wawona and audit the books," Marjorie said. Since all the Washburn brothers "paid bills out of their own pockets, tossed large sums of cash in an unlocked drawer and kept accounts in their heads if they did not forget entirely," Jay Cook spent days before he "finally arrived at a trial balance which was only $7.75 short. All the Washburns thought that was wonderful and were distinctly annoyed when Dad refused $7.75 out of a pocket and insisted on looking for what he called an error.

"Only my Indian friends knew better stories than Uncle Harry. No one loved a joke more than he did. He could still laugh if the joke was on him, and no one was kinder. When he died [October 25, 1902], half of Mariposa County wore invisible mourning." After his death, Marjorie claimed that "Wawona's greatest charm always was that the Sentinel Hotel in My Semty Valley was only twenty-six miles over the mountain."

One of the results of the Roosevelt-Muir camping trip was the president's strong support of the recession of the Yosemite Valley and Mariposa Grove Grant from the state of California to the federal government. Thereafter those two unique areas were part of Yosemite National Park. State pride and politics delayed the actual change of administration until August 1, 1906, when the Yosemite Valley Commissioners had to surrender the Grant and, incidentally, their jobs and power, to the United States.

Until the advent of the National Park Service, cavalry troops would be the guardians as they already were in the rest of the National Park system. Their commander, Major H. C. Benson, served as acting superintendent of the park, and the troopers' camp was set up on the site where Yosemite Lodge was later built.

Despite the fact that Marjorie did not mention the change of administration in her manuscript, it had an immediate impact on her life. Realizing that his job would end when the army took over the power plant, Charlie Atkinson decided to go into ranching near Santa Cruz. Just prior to the family's departure, Dorothy and Marjorie "reviewed our past and despaired of our future." As adults, however, their friendship was renewed.

After the Yosemite Valley Railroad established a terminus at El Portal, the Cooks rode what Marjorie called "the noisy thing" on trips to San Francisco. Since the Valley was no longer so isolated, they could spend at least part of the winter at the Sentinel. After Marjorie's graduation from grammar school, in 1907, she attended boarding school, but did not specify where, when, or how long in her narrative.

Camp Curry's success with tent "camping" at two dollars a day and no tipping—versus $3.50

to $5.00 a day plus tips at the Sentinel—soon in-spired competition. In 1901 Jay Cook established Camp Yosemite (later renamed Camp Lost Arrow) on a flat near the base of Lower Yosemite Fall. Although each unit had a manager, Cook was in overall charge there, at the Sentinel, and at the Glacier Point Hotel. A third tent camp, Camp Ahwahnee, was set up a mile west of the Sentinel in 1908 by Cook's old friend Will Sell. Tourism had proliferated because of rail service, so competition was not too hurtful to the Sentinel.

In 1908 Cook was appointed postmaster for Yosemite Valley, which pleased Marjorie. "When we wintered in Yosemite, the post office moved to our [Ivy] Cottage. I liked that arrangement." Equipment consisting of a chair, counter, and pigeon-holed cupboard did not take up much room, and Marjorie was "acting postmaster. Three times a week, the arriving mail gave me an opportunity to visit with at least one member of every [resident] family. It also gave me a chance to read several funnies as papers of summer residents often continued to come most of the winter. After I finished they made the rounds ending at deserted Kenneyville where [winter caretaker] John Babtiste Bachagalupi perused them by lonely candle light. My St. Nichols and Dorothy's Youth's Companion also circulated."

When the Cooks were away, storekeeper Nelson Salter "became temporary winter postmaster. He said it was good for business. People shopped and sometimes settled their accounts while they waited for the mail to arrive."

Mail delivery greatly improved with the advent of the shortline railroad, since it was carried by train, not horseback, to El Portal, then loaded aboard a stage for the final run into Yosemite Valley. When the road was blocked by snow, a man on horseback took over as in earlier years.

A few days before Christmas 1910, Cook received notification that his appointment as postmaster would not be renewed. That, on top of other concerns, upset him emotionally as well as physically. Even though it was snowless, Christmas day was particularly festive because Marjorie had three friends as guests. After dinner, Cook joined a ball game in front of the hotel before going in to his private office after five o'clock. A few minutes later, the *Merced Sun* reported, "a shot was heard and the porter of the hotel rushed in and found Mr. Cook dead."

An inquest, conducted by Gabriel Sovulewski on December 26, determined that Jay Bruce Cook's suicide by gunshot had been due to "temporary insanity caused by brooding over his ill health and irregularities in his business affairs." Within a short time, Will Sell, Jr. took over Cook's leases and responsibilities.

Marjorie Cook's "childhood of enchantment" was over, and she and her mother moved to Berkeley. Little else is known about Marjorie except that she married a man surnamed Wilson, and was living in Berkeley when she wrote a 50,000-word autobiography of her youth in Yosemite Valley. It was written for publication under the name of Jayne Bruce, a typed copy of which was given to the Yosemite Research Library. This manuscript, although rambling and unedited, has been a treasure trove to the author in recreating part of Yosemite's past.

6

Village Youths

ON July 28, 1901 Marjorie Cook and Dorothy Atkinson witnessed a romantic wedding near the base of Bridalveil Fall. In fact, Marjorie recalled, they "nearly fell in Pohono's pool in our efforts to get close to the fascinating bride who did not so much as scowl at us when we inadvertently headed the wedding procession."

Tall, slender Anne Rippey with "rosy cheeks and bright eyes," was twenty-two when, after a two-month courtship, she married artist Harry C. Best, a big, broad-shouldered man fifteen years her senior. "They started their honeymoon in a big stage decorated with tin cans and old shoes amid a shower of rice and sand supplied by Dorothy and me," Marjorie related. "We had dropped our bag of rice and the sand got mixed quite by accident. The very new Mrs. Best was a good sport even though we half smothered her."

Sadly, the bride's spirit was quelled during the honeymoon at the Wawona Hotel. Pneumonia followed her soaking in a thunderstorm, and although she regained her élan vital, her lungs were permanently damaged.

In 1902, after receiving a permit from the Yosemite Valley Commissioners to operate a "studio," the couple set up shop in a tent in Yosemite Village. While Anne sold Harry's paintings, and photographs taken and printed by Putnam and Valentine, a Los Angeles firm, Harry continued to paint Yosemite scenes. Within a year or so a small structure housed Best's Studio. The Bests spent winters in San Francisco.

Virginia Rose Best's birth in January 1904 furthered weakened Anne, but her delight and

Virginia Best's parents were married at the base of Bridalveil Fall, and ever since her birth in 1904 her life and allegiance have been involved with Yosemite. (Virginia Best Adams (VBA) Collection)

Harry's pride in the child were enormous, then and later. When Virginia was only sixteen months old, her father said, "I don't think she will ever be very bad like some children." And she wasn't!

During a 1992 interview with the author about her childhood, Virginia Best Adams explained that "I went to school all year long because in Yosemite it began in April and I got there in May, and then I left in late October."

For several years they traveled by train from Merced to El Portal. As author Hank Johnston later claimed, it was a "Shortline to Paradise," but the seventy-eight clickety-clack miles were not a pleasure trip. Virginia recalled that "It was very hot coming up the canyon and, of course, there was no air conditioning. They [the Yosemite Valley Railroad Company] had it fixed originally so that you had to stay overnight at the Del Portal Hotel. That was the first time I ever saw anybody drunk. Mother said, 'Just ignore them.'

"We stayed the night, and the next morning we came up on the stage. When we got to Cascade Fall, the driver stopped and gave us drinks of water in a tin cup. I'm sure that stop was so the horses could rest."

After automobiles were allowed in Yosemite Valley, Harry Best bought a Ford, and altered the front passenger seat so that "Mother and I could sleep in the car." By then the Bests lived in San Diego, where Harry had a winter studio. "It took half a day to pack up," Virginia recalled, so their first camping night usually was at Capistrano, the next at Los Angeles, "and Mother had a sister in Santa Barbara."

When asked about her favorite place in Yosemite, Virginia's answer was immediate and enthusiastic: "I loved it all. And I had such excitement each year seeing Bridalveil Fall, Yosemite Falls and all that. It could be 1910, 1912, 1914, it didn't make any difference, I love it all still!

"Once we got to the Village, it was hard work for my father because our place had been closed up all winter and he had to put it together, uncover the skylights, and make a fire in the wood stove." Best's Studio was one room with a skylight, facing the stage road, the fourth building up from the general store. In between stood Boysen's Studio, operated by Daniel and Mabel Boysen; Yosemite Falls Studio, run by printer and publish-er D. J. Foley; and the guardian's office and home. Best's Studio, as were the other buildings, was longer than it was wide, and was backed by a meadow and the Merced River. Small back rooms or separate buildings or tents served as living quarters for the concessionaires.

"Our dining room had a skylight, and I bet that was the original studio," Virginia explained. "Every year, Dad would get permission to add on and get closer to the road."

Virginia was proud of the studio where her father's paintings were permanently displayed, one on an easel, many on the walls, still others leaning against the baseboards. A small organ, a sofa, burl slabs, deer skins, and antlers added to the rustic decor.

Sales depended primarily on visitors who arrived by stage on Raymond-Whitcomb tours and stayed at the Sentinel Hotel. Up to forty-four in a group, squeezed into a series of stages, were welcomed by hotel manager Jay Cook and other local businessmen. A rainy day was equally welcome, since the visitors, instead of seeing the sights, were more likely to browse and buy. On a showery day in May 1905, for example, Best took in twelve dollars from sales of Putnam and Valentine prints.

Best, understandably, preferred selling one of his own paintings, on which prices ranged from fifteen dollars to seventy-five dollars., including frames he had made. To augment his skimpy income, he painted signs. His own, displayed inside the hotel, read: "Tourists are cordially invited to visit Bests Studio and inspect his paintings of Yosemite. Oils & watercolors. A full line of artists proofs, platinum and sepia prints."

Best was enthusiastic about his landscapes. "Darling," he wrote his wife in May 1905, "I have made the most beautiful Mirror Lake ever. Everybody who has seen it is raving. Winding road and the real color of the rocks. Lavender, full of golden sun. It delights the eye."

Virginia remembered that her father sketched a scene before working on a painting, and that he was patient with observers and was "very nice" to them. His stature as an artist increased as sales and exhibits enlarged his reputation.

En route to Italy for study in the winter of 1907, Best had an exhibit at the Cosmos Club in

36

Washington, D.C. After a private showing for President Theodore Roosevelt, the Bests were invited to the White House, where three-year-old Virginia so charmed the president that he held her on his lap and gave her a signed photograph of his family.

As she grew older, Virginia enjoyed the annual Yosemite events, such as "Memorial Day when the school children put flowers on the graves in the cemetery. And Fourth of July when all the buildings were decorated with flags and buntings, and the soldiers shot off rockets and firecrackers in the evening. Perhaps we had a parade and a picnic, or an Indian Field Day horseback tug-of-war and potato races, prizes for the best baskets and babies, and hand games in the Indian Village."

High water in the spring was annoying to adults, but exciting for children. Virginia remembered that "woodpiles on the edge of the meadow

This winsome picture of Virginia Best and Arthur Pillsbury in front, Grace Pillsbury, Billie Garrett, Ellen Boysen, and Ernest Pillsbury in back may have been taken by pioneer photographer George Fiske about 1913. His studio in the Village is in the background. (VBA Collection)

behind the houses in the village had to be staked down so that they wouldn't float away during the night, and after school the children made rafts and paddled through the grassy pools."

Asked if her family went to the Sentinel for meals, Virginia replied, "No, in the first place we couldn't afford it, and in the second place, the Jorgensens went quite regularly and he [Chris Jorgensen] and Dad didn't get along very well." Jorgensen, established in the Valley as resident artist since 1899, resented competition and disdained Best's work.

In contrast, the Boysens, who ran a photographic shop just down the road, had attended Anne and Harry's wedding, and were good neighbors. Their only child, Ellen, loved baby Virginia. Later, Ellen "dominated," Virginia said, since she "was three years older; the one that made all the decisions. When we [the village children] used to play after dinner, we would play hide-and-go-seek outside. Daddy [John] Degnan used to sort of supervise us all, and he would be my partner."

By then Marjorie Cook was a remote teenager, and the Atkinsons had left Yosemite. Most of the Degnan children were grown, but Ruth, born in 1895, and little Alice, born in 1902, were among the village gang. A girl named Billie Garrett, who usually spent the summer with Ellen Boysen, completed the group. Because the Sovulewskis lived on the other side of the Valley, Virginia said, "we didn't really see them very much." Grace Sovulewski, then attending school in Pasadena, later became Virginia's best friend.

Kitty Dexter was Virginia's first teacher, but Ora Boring, who taught from 1911 to 1914, was her favorite. Miss Boring, a former science teacher at Stanford, shared her knowledge and enthusiasm for birds, flowers, and forests with her pupils, encouraging them to observe and appreciate nature. Virginia remembered that "The first student who saw a robin or the first wildflower of the season would tell about it in school, but Mr. Sovulewski [a member of the school board] didn't like that because he felt she ought to concentrate on reading, 'riting, and 'rithmetic." Miss Boring corresponded with Virginia long after she had left Yosemite.

After the Stoneman House burned, in 1896, an abandoned stage office—near where the LeConte Memorial Lodge was erected in 1903—was utilized as a schoolhouse. In 1909 or 1910 it was moved to a site across the river. That was the school Virginia attended, sometimes riding her father's old bicycle there and back. Other times she walked back and forth twice, because she went home for lunch. Playground equipment was scant, but "there was an iron bar, which was probably used to tie horses, and I remember we used to go over and over it."

The fifty-year-old apple orchard planted by Hutchings was a short stroll away. In the fall, Virginia said, "We walked over to pick apples, and put two or three in our bloomer leg. At school we would put them in our desks, then lean down occasionally to get bites." Presumably the teacher's back was turned, and recitations from pupils muffled the sounds of chewing.

After 1916, when the short-lived Desmond Company had 200 laborers excavate for a basement and build a 1,500-foot foundation wall for a never-built hotel west of the school, the pupils delighted in walking around the foundation. "He [Desmond] didn't get very far you know," explained Virginia. "I don't remember what the inside size was, but we didn't have any fear of falling into a deep place."

A few Indian children attended school, but Old Mary was the first Indian woman Virginia really knew, and "Alice James was a very good friend. And there was also Lena Brown who married John Brown." Two of the sons of that union were named after Chris Jorgensen and his son Virgil.

There were three major events in Yosemite during the first decades of the twentieth century: the recession of the 1864 Yosemite Grant that resulted in its becoming part of Yosemite National Park under the administration of the army; the 1916 founding of the National Park Service and the beginning of civilian administration; and the First World War. Virginia was an infant when the army took over, and thus remembered nothing about it except that the acting superintendent's residence was next door, and that Major Forsyth's daughter Dorothy was another of the group of village children during his 1909–1912 tenure.

Dorothy "had a horse," Virginia commented, "and none of the rest of us had horses." Sometimes she got to ride.

Usually "Winkey" carried gear, but in this instance Pillsbury photographed his niece Grace and his nephews Arthur and Ernest on board. (Melinda Pillsbury-Foster Collection)

got to borrow some. I had a *wonderful* time!" Her interest in California history and book collecting was sparked by his library.

Virginia recalled the false armistice in November 1917. "When we heard that the war was over, we all celebrated and drove around the Valley tooting the horns. Then we found it was a mistake and not the real thing so when the real one came a bit later, it was kind of an anticlimax. I remember we had a Red Cross group and people did bandages and knitting. Mrs. Sovulewski was one of the active ones."

Anne Best's prematurely white hair enhanced her beauty, but she was increasingly fragile and died of tuberculosis in 1920 at age forty-one. Although often ill, she had been a radiant, greatly-loved person.[1] "It must have been hard on my father to have the responsibility of a teenager," Virginia commented. "He hired a cook and maybe there would be two girls working in the studio. I didn't do much in the shop until I was out of high school."

Sometime during the following summer, naturalist Ansel Hall brought a lean, enthusiastic young man into the studio, saying, Virginia recalled, "I'd like you to meet a friend." The friend was Ansel Adams, the twenty-year-old custodian of the Sierra Club's lodge. Virginia was seventeen, and at first didn't remember his name. "It took us a little while to get acquainted."

When the "Major saw my [Virginia's] cat chase after a gray squirrel, he said 'no more cats in the Valley.'"

After the National Park Service rangers took over in 1916, Virginia met rangers in both the protective and naturalist branches. "The first ranger I really knew was Park naturalist Ansel Hall, and he had a little trunk full of books, and I

Harry Best let Ansel practice what Ansel termed "uproarious scales and Debussian dissonances" on the piano. The two young people became friends and more, but they weren't married until 1927. Both loved music—Ansel planned to be a pianist—exploring the high country and, indeed, all of Yosemite.

Virginia's first climbing experience was with

---

1. Only one of the two eastern maple trees that Anne Rippey Best planted near Best's Studio still stands, but each fall its red-leafed glory thrills residents and visitors.

Enid and Charlie Michael. He was assistant postmaster and a climber, and she was such an ardent naturalist that she wrote columns on nature for publication. Their summer residence was a tent they pitched "on what we called Rowe Island up the river above Sentinel Bridge. We had to persuade my father to let me go. Until then I had done nothing, but, after I knew the Michaels, nature meant far more to me."

In June of 1912 the Village "gang" was increased by photographer Arthur C. Pillsbury's nephews Ernest, then thirteen, Arthur, age seven, and niece Grace, eleven. They had been injured and their parents killed the preceding September in an automobile accident. After that they lived with their Uncle Arthur and Aunt Aetheline in Oakland and, seasonally, in Yosemite Valley, where Arthur maintained a photographic studio.

Photographer Arthur C. Pillsbury and artist Harry C. Best relaxing after a hard morning's work. (VBA Collection)

In 1978, Grace recalled that "Our first trip to Yosemite was 1912," by train. "Uncle met us at El Portal the next morning with his horse and cart. My aunt went to U.C. summer school. I think she needed a rest from us. That was the only year we attended 'school' in Yosemite." Virginia Best, Ellen Boysen, and her friend Billie Garrett met, Grace said, "at the Pavilion in the mornings for a month where we studied nature with the school teacher. There were field trips where we gathered flowers to press in the Pavilion. We also learned about the birds and took two trips with Dr. [François] Matthes who was camped at El Capitan Bridge near the terminal moraine. One trip was to the medial moraine between Happy Isles and Mirror Lake."

In June 1914, "Uncle," as the children called him, was unable to meet them at El Portal, and they missed the bus to the Valley. "Finally, we got tired of waiting," Art explained years later, "and started walking, each carrying his suitcase. When we did not arrive on the bus, Uncle started telephoning, and learned that we had been seen passing the electric hydro-generating station at Cascade Falls. Uncle got on his horse, and started down the road after us, meeting us a bit northeast of Pohono Bridge. Grace and I rode, and carried the suitcases. Uncle and Ernest walked."

That year was pivotal in Yosemite history, because civilian rangers had replaced U. S. Cavalry troops in patrolling the Park, and automobiles were coexisting with horsedrawn vehicles.

Pillsbury's Studio stood west of Degnan's and close to the Yosemite Chapel. His family and employees, including a cook, were housed in scattered tents. A lean-to back of the store served as kitchen and dining room. Art never forgot the time when "We arrived on May first, a bit earlier than usual. That night I could think of nothing better than to sleep under the stars. In the morning I awoke only to find myself covered with two inches of snow, and you can bet I was wild with excitement. I also remember one spring when there were particularly heavy floods. Many people were flooded out, and Yosemite Falls, in chocolate brown color, roared incessantly."

Pillsbury was an energetic, innovative man, ready to try even a hot air balloon so as to take unique photographs. He had hauled his camera gear around Alaska and the Yukon in 1898 and 1899 during the Klondike Gold Rush. By 1914 he was a pioneer in taking movies of Yosemite, and showing them on the studio's porch at night. He had a twenty- by fifty-foot porch added to the studio to accommodate spectators.

"There were usually big crowds at the free movies," Art said. "The studio was always open afterwards, and that was the busy time of the day, with the cash register ringing merrily."

Art suspected that "Uncle's" effective narration accompanying his movies was rehearsed, but "we never witnessed it." Art did witness Pillsbury's perfectionism in constantly taking new pictures, and trying new film and filters. His adopted children were often involved in carrying equipment. Art remembered hazardous trips up the back of Half Dome, pulling himself along by clutching the inch-thick rope, his fearless, sure-footed uncle "off at the side taking pictures." Steel cables were installed three feet apart in 1919. "That meant a return trip, with more climbers—more and better action.

"There were rather frequent trips over the Pohono Trail, as different wild flowers were in bloom at different times of the year. There were trips up the Long Trail to Glacier Point. There was a trip up the side of Yosemite Falls, and over the top of El Capitan. When an old mining road was reopened as the Tioga Road, we went over it, taking pictures all the way," in one of a series of Studebakers that Pillsbury wore out.

"Uncle," however, was not the first to take his adopted children on a camping trip. Instead, Art said, their neighbor, kindly John Degnan, "utilized his vacation to take us kids camping near the Merced River in Little Yosemite. We walked, and had Uncle's donkey 'Winkey' to carry our gear and food. On the camping trip, there were us three Pillsbury kids, Ellen Boysen and a boy cousin of hers, Virginia Best, and the Degnan children. The boys were Chris and John." The girls, Ruth and Alice.

In either 1914 or 1915, "Mrs. Degnan started serving ice cream on her front porch," Art continued. "An ice house was built in the back of her house, and, in winter, ice was sawed from Mirror Lake, and stored in the ice house with sawdust. A small herd of cows was in a small enclosure (fenced) out of sight in Bridal Veil meadows. There was no pasteurization of the milk. Either Chris or John would go down in the morning in the pick-up truck and milk the cows, and return in the evening for the second milking. There was a large ice cream freezer in the front of the ice

house, and I would often help a little turning the crank on the freezer, and I would be rewarded with licking of the paddle after the boy had salvaged all he could."

Grace remembered an Indian Field Days during which "There was an Indian Dance where they went around a circle in full costume (probably furnished by the Lodge and thought up by them).[2] The younger Indians would laugh so hard they could hardly sing."

Both Grace and Art remembered Pillsbury's first Studebaker Big Six touring car, which he purchased when automobiles were first allowed on the Big Oak Flat Road, late in the 1914 season. Before the road was opened the following spring, "Uncle was off to the Big Oak Flat Road with some strong bodies to help him. And plenty of shovels. In due time, Uncle reached the Valley to win a cup that the Desmond Company, I think, awarded the first car in. Needless to say there was a lot of publicity."

By 1916, "Uncle decided there must be some easier way. So he secretly got permission from the Yosemite Valley Railroad to go up the tracks." Pillsbury had special rims made with flanges that fit the tracks, but "They proved too light; so they put the tires back on" and bumped across the ties to El Portal. I still have the cup (silver) which says that they reached the Valley on April 10, 1916. This incident greatly improved the publicity for the Studebaker Big Six, and it wasn't long before we had a new car (presented by the dealer)." Grace added that Pillsbury had a regular siren horn, and "When he arrived at the Sentinel Hotel at 11:00 P.M., Uncle gave a blast on the siren. Chief Ranger Forest Townsley remarked, 'That sounds like Pillsbury.' Later he appropriated the siren for his car."

By 1918, Ernest, the older brother, had joined the army, and Grace was in high school, but all through his high school and college years Art spent summers taking adventurous, axle-breaking trips with Uncle, and running off thousands of Pillsbury's postcards on primitive machines. "There was one machine that would expose the cards, one roll at a time . . . a separate system that would develop, rinse, fix, and wash the cards . . .

2. At that time, Yosemite Lodge was a concession operated by the short-lived Desmond Park Service Company.

a mimeograph machine that would print the usual 'post office' information on the rear in blocks of three each. Many cards were ruined."

Another adventurous lad was Hart Cook, Jr. He was twelve when his mother, Ellen C. Cook, became manager of the Sentinel Hotel late in October of 1917.[3] His father, a retired fire chief, was to be storeroom manager. Once again Cooks reigned at the Sentinel, but they were not related to the Jay Bruce Cooks.

Their nighttime arrival coincided with a full moon, which the boy never forgot. "The magnificent rugged cliffs encircling the valley and outlined against the star-studded sky looked ghost-like under the moon. I also could see the towering pines that reached up forever and the places where the dwindling waterfalls of the autumn season still trickled down." His description and other quotations are taken from the 1990 book, *My Mother, the Chef*, by Hart—who died in 1989—and his wife, Beth.

During Hart's explorations the next day, he was particularly impressed with Cedar Cottage. Beside the tree that pierced the roof above the lobby, originally Hutchings' kitchen, he spotted a pool table and a player piano. Later he said, "My musical accomplishments on the player piano astounded even me."

His excitement diminished when he had to don "short britches with bands just below the knees. These bands buckled tightly to hold up long stockings." Ankle-high leather shoes, a long-sleeved, ironed shirt, jacket, and flat- topped cap, atop neatly-combed hair, completed his going-to-school outfit.

After forty years of seasonal sessions, the Yosemite School had gone on regular terms in 1916. Hart was not impressed with the one-room structure, nor with his two sixth-grade classmates, Gabe (Gabrielle) Sovulewski and Donna Solinsky, both of them daughters of Park Service employees. He learned quickly that "children from government families usually did not mix with those of company families. As a result, a young lad growing up in Yosemite, I had very

few children to play with since I was the only one who had 'company' parents.

"The delightful exception to this odd caste system were the Sovulewski 'kids.'" After Hart discovered a seemingly ownerless rowboat behind the Sentinel, he enlisted the boys as crew. "Bob Sovulewski, being the biggest, became the engineer. He manipulated the oars. Joe, being next in size, posed as a deck hand, while Tom, the smallest, took the part of the ship's cook, providing us with apples, most of them too green to eat. I appointed myself captain and pilot. Naturally!

"We took that rowboat upstream and down in an area of about 100 yards including going under Sentinel Bridge. High water or low, the condition of the river did not faze us."

Unluckily for Hart, Clara M. Hodges, the strict teacher, who later became Yosemite's first woman ranger, lived at the Sentinel. "Sometimes during the evenings when I lingered around the [lobby] stove with older people, Miss Hodges would ask, 'Hart, have you done your homework?'

"She would peer through her glasses as if she could read minds. That proved scary since some of my thoughts pertained to her."

Aside from school, "Winter meant snow plows, roughly made creations consisting of heavy timbers forming a triangle with its point at the front. Large rocks filled the inside area for weight. All this was pulled by horses."

Winter guests traveled by train to El Portal and then by motorized stage to the Sentinel. Business picked up for a festive, homey Christmas. "When the colored lights went up in the hotel and along the upper deck and garlands of fragrant fresh pine and cedar draped the walls I could not contain my excitement," Hart remembered. "Outside a tall pine tree would glow with more lights amid the snow."

Ice skating on the river or, if the ice there wasn't thick enough, on a shallow frozen pond back of the chapel, was a popular sport, as were making snowmen or engaging in snowball fights. Nevertheless, Hart was joyful "when the winters (and school) were over." After he found a large

---

3. Ellen Cook had been hired by the Yosemite National Park Company to manage its massive Del Portal Hotel. Unfortunately, it burned the night before she arrived. Because T. E. Farrow, general manager for the Company, was badly injured in the fire, William Sell, Jr., the Sentinel's manager, was sent to San Francisco to replace him, and Mrs. Cook took Sell's place.

boulder behind Cedar Cottage pockmarked with mortar cups, he tried to imagine generations of Indian women grinding acorns thousands of times to create the deep impressions.

Part of his trouble, he realized, was that the only Indian he knew was a half-breed named Pete Hilliard. "Pete sported a beautiful Pancho Villa mustache and drove a big truck to El Portal to meet the train. If there were any tourists arriving he would take one of the passenger buses, and transport those people and supplies that had come in on the train.

"People in the Valley would phone in their grocery orders to the [Village] store and when Pete got back from El Portal he would deliver them." Pete's method of teaching Hart to drive a 1914 White truck "with an H shift and square box transmission," was unorthodox but practical.

"I would ride with him on his grocery deliveries and he would let me take the wheel. But the moment I let the gears clatter, 'Stop,' he would say. 'Get out,' he would say." And the crestfallen boy would have to plod home to the hotel no matter what the weather or distance.

By the age of fourteen, although unlicensed, Hart was proficient enough to be hired to drive the Company's "shuttle bus," another 1914 White. His uniform was boots or puttees, riding pants, long-sleeved shirt, and genuine Stetson hat, and his pay a munificent six dollars a day—high wages for the time.

His first job, a year earlier, was even more romantic: Postmaster Fred Alexander hired him to deliver telegrams to campers via horseback. "A message would come addressed simply to So-and-So in Camp Seven for instance. I would go to the camp and keep asking until I found the rightful person."

On winter weekends Mrs. Cook put Hart to work on the hotel's switchboard. These jobs were the first of a parade of work in and out of the Park for the versatile Hart.

From 1906 on, Sovulewski children, grandchildren, and, until recently, great-grandchildren have grown up in Yosemite. Their tenure began with Rose and Gabriel Sovulewski—she a New Englander, he Polish. After a decade of service with the U. S. Cavalry, part of it in Yosemite National Park, ex-Sergeant Sovulewski returned in 1906 to work for the government, eventually becoming supervisor of roads and trails.

At first the family lived partly in army tents and partly in the deteriorating Hutchings cabin, which Sovulewski pronounced as "unfit for human habitation."[4] Finally the government allocated $2,800 for a new house, and Sovulewski himself put in about $800 to install plumbing, wiring, and essential fixtures. The finished six-bedroom, two-story house lacked any architectural merit, and blocked one of the best views of Yosemite Falls, but to the Sovulewskis, including five children—Grace, Lawrence, Mildred, Gabrielle, and infant Robert—the house seemed palatial when they moved in sometime in 1910. Joseph, born in 1911, and Thomas, born in 1913, completed the lively brood. It was the youngest boys who "crewed" for Hart Cook.

Their freedom was restricted only by the then nearby school—whose teacher sometimes boarded with the Sovulewskis—and the expectations of their strict parents. Nevertheless, the three girls remembered childhood as an enchanting time of riding horseback and then letting their horses graze in the meadow, either ice skating on or swimming in the Merced River, and, best of all, camping in the high country. Sovulewski maintained a base camp in Tuolumne Meadows, which overflowed with children, guests, and noise.

The girls rode horses with their dad as he surveyed routes and supervised trail building, reveling in the myriad beauties of nature. Although Sovulewski resisted having any place named for him, his oldest daughters were proud to have Grace Meadow and Mildred Lake given their names.

All the boys became proficient fishermen, particularly Tom whose favorite spots were Tuolumne Meadows and Merced Lake. "Why," he recalled, fishing was so good at the lake, you'd have to get behind a tree to tie a fly or they'd come and get it."

When Jay Bruce, the State Lion Hunter, rescued three orphaned lion cubs in April 1918, Chief Ranger Townsley gave them to the

---

4. It was torn down in 1909 or 1910.

Sovulewski family to raise. "My mother raised 'em," Tom claimed, "feeding them with baby bottles, lying on their backs in a row. I guess they got their pictures taken about a hundred times."

Mildred remembered the lion kittens galloping through the house, and making "music" by racing up and down on the piano keys. Bob, Joe, and Tom delighted in hiding the cubs behind trees, then letting them jump out to frighten tourists.

By the time the cubs were three months old they were so big and fierce that they had to be caged—"put on exhibition," Bruce reported, "with a cash box beside the cage, bringing in some $5,000 for the Red Cross," before the end of World War I.[5]

Later, a couple of bear cubs were added to the impromptu, unsightly zoo. Two of the lions died from lack of raw meat, and two bears were released. But other orphaned or injured wild animals were "protected" by well-meaning rangers—partly as a means of educating the public.

Even in the late 1920s Sovulewski's young granddaughter, Margaret Anne Taylor, tagged along to watch him dump a large pot of oatmeal inside the fence. No one else was allowed to enter. About that time, the authorities ruled that survival of the fittest, rather than survival by sanctuary, should ensue, and the zoo was eliminated.[6]

As they matured, the Sovulewski kids sought work in the Park. Like Hart Cook, Tom's first job was delivering telegrams for Fred Alexander, who was the telegraph operator as well as the postmaster. Subsequently, Tom washed dishes at the Ahwahnee Hotel, and worked six-day weeks for one of his dad's trail crews. Although none of the boys stayed in Yosemite, all three girls did for years. Grace married Frank Ewing, who followed his father-in-law's lead in doing trail, road, and civic work. Mildred wed Lawrence Taylor, who was with the CCC during the Depression and eventually worked for the Curry Company. Mildred worked in Best's Studio until she retired in 1972, the year the studio was renamed The

Gabrielle Sovulewski with a lapful of lion.
(Keith Walker Collection)

Ansel Adams Gallery. Gabrielle became a champion skier, worked for the Company, and married its hotel executive, George Goldsworthy. They were childless, but the Ewings raised two

---

5. See *Cougar Killer* by Jay C. Bruce, pp. 134-35. (Comet Press, 1953.)

6. See *Yosemite: The Embattled Wilderness,* by Alfred Runte, pp. 133–34. (Lincoln: University of Nebraska Press, 1990.)

children, Herb and Charlotte, who continued the Sovulewski dynasty of living and working in the Park. Margaret Anne and Nancy Taylor also spent part of their married lives in the Park.

Just as Ellen Boysen, Virginia Best, Hart Cook, the three Pillsburys, the Solinskys, and various Degnans did, the Sovulewski clan retained a lifetime of love and allegiance to Yosemite.

One of the many fish that didn't get away from Tom Sovulewski was this 26-inch long German brown trout that weighed over eight pounds. Tom said he was using a split bamboo pole with a black and brown fly on a #14 hook on a heavy leader. (Thomas Sovulewski Collection)

7

In the Footsteps of John Muir

O N OUR FOURTH TRIP IN THE SIERRA, my brother and I decided to go to the Yosemite region, the grandest place on earth, where all kinds of mountains are available with wonderful trout fishing." So began the account of a trip that John Muir's eldest grandson, Strentzel Hanna, kept between June 21 and August 29, 1919. Although it wasn't his first summer in the Sierra, and he did not write with anything like the eloquence of his famous grandfather, who had died in 1914, the journal was remarkable, for its adventuring author was barely thirteen years old.

Strentzel, named for his maternal grandfather, John T. Strentzel, had been born on June 20, 1906, and his companion on the trip, his brother John, on March 16, 1909. Muir's daughter, Wanda Muir Hanna, and her husband, Thomas Rea Hanna, a mining engineer turned farmer, were the parents of four sons and a daughter; a fifth son was born in 1920. The family home was an old adobe near the Strentzel-Muir home, now the John Muir National Historic Site.

In contrast to Muir, who had been an overprotective father, Wanda and Tom were almost permissive, and had such confidence in their sons, daughter Jean Hanna Clark stated, that they "went on pack trips in the Sierra unchaperoned except for their animals . . . stopping at farmhouses and sleeping in barns or camping along the way." By 1919, Strent and John were trusted and trustworthy, and were allowed, if not actively encouraged, to travel. At a time when travel dangers were at a minimum, the two youngsters rode horseback to Yosemite in the footsteps of grandfather Muir.

Later, Strent revised his scribbled trip account for a school theme, which must have received an A. It was appreciated for its uniqueness and modesty by his wife, Edna Sheriden Hanna, and, later, by two sons and a daughter—Jim, David, and Susan.

Until this book, devoted to children's adventures and perceptions, Strent's journal has never been published—as it is now with the kind permission of his children. Condensation was necessary and background material has been added, but little other editing was done.

"Every good mountaineer starts getting ready

John Muir would have been proud of his grandsons for their 1919 summer in the Sierra, a half century after his first adventuring in many of the same places. (YRL Collection)

months ahead of time," Strent began his narrative, "so we started fixing up our old fishing rods by re-wrapping them and varnishing them . . . making some 'jerkey' and getting the outfit together. Our outfit was as follows:

> 3 horses, 2 saddle and 1 pack.
> 1 pack saddle.
> 2 pack beds.
> 1 double bed.
> fire irons (for cooking).
> 1 pack rope.
> 1 pack cinch.
> supplies.

In addition, they carried extra already-fitted horseshoes. "Our tools for shoeing were 1 camp axe (small) to clinch nails against, 1 horse shoe hammer, 1 pair nippers, to cut nails, 1 rasp, to level the hoof. Besides these, we used the butcher knife to help cut down the hoof."

A day after Strent's thirteenth birthday, the brothers mounted their horses, Victorina and Bethel, led Buck, the pack horse, and rode to Crockett on the Carquinez Strait, where they boarded ship for the trip up the San Joaquin River to Stockton. Even then the sight of two young boys traveling alone must have occasioned comment, but Strent no more mentioned that than he noted any last minute admonitions from his parents. Nowhere in his account did Strent betray any homesickness on either his or John's part. They must have exchanged letters with, and probably received money from, their parents, but Strent did not mention such things. However, their father was in Yosemite Valley for at least part of the time that they were there. François Matthes, the noted geologist, wrote in his diary that he had dinner in Yosemite Valley on July 1

John Muir Hanna on his pony. Photo by François Matthes at Young Lake on July 26, 1919. (Courtesy, The Bancroft Library)

with Tom Hanna and Professor William F. Badè, who gave a lecture that evening on the life of John Muir.

From Stockton they rode twenty-eight miles southeast to a farm near Modesto. A farmer charged them a dollar for their night's lodging on the edge of a wind-breaking haystack. Packing Buck demanded strength as well as ingenuity, since the boys were still short in stature and the packs heavy. "When they were heavy," Strent explained, "we would lift one up together, when it was high enough I would hold it on my shoulder while John would go around on the other side of the horse and hook the straps over the saddle. The second bag was always the hardest to put on because the first bag would turn the saddle. Our bed went on top of the bags and the fire irons, axe and bucket on top of all.

"We use the Basque hitch. It is easy to throw and is particularly good because it tightens around the bags as you travel and loosens under the horse's belly. The Diamond and other hitches do not do this but loosen up easily and let the pack slip."

Their third night was at La Grange, where they "bought a loaf of bread and some canned beans which we ate for supper and breakfast. Our bill amounted to about three dollars, including horse feed.

"From La Grange to Coulterville was a long and hot day's ride," Strent wrote, and there they "met an old stagedriver who knew the family. He talked half the night about old times when he used to drive stages." 'Old times' was only a few years back, inasmuch as automobiles had not been allowed into Yosemite via the Coulterville Road until 1913, and via the Big Oak Flat and Wawona roads until 1914. In fact, stages had operated on the latter route until April of 1916.

"In the morning we traveled [via the Coulterville Road] to Bower Cave where we had dinner," Strent recorded on June 26. Afterwards a guide led them down a long flight of steep steps into what appeared to be more of a pit than a cave. It has a small lake in the bottom, "and the reflection of the sky above made many beautiful colors." Skepticism was strong in the practical youth: "The guide said the cave was 240 feet deep, but his stories were all too big to believe." Muir's description fifty years earlier, when he was nearly triple his grandson's age, was more poetic: "It has a fine clear little lake," he wrote, "with mossy banks embowered with broad-leaf maples, all under ground."

Darkness forced them to camp along the road. "The next morning we got up early and with Yosemite only a few [eighteen] miles away, started out and had not gone more than a quarter of a mile when we came to Hazel Green which is nothing more than a beautiful meadow, a barn, and a house.

"We, as well as the horses, were tired and hungry from the night before, so did not travel very fast. The road was very steep and we went over several ridges thinking that from the top of each ridge we would get our first glimpse of Yosemite. Finally we saw a large sign which read 'First glimpse of the Yosemite and its domes.' It was from here that we saw Half Dome, El Capitan, Three Brothers, and nearly all the domes. We also saw Bridal Veil Falls.

"It was about one o'clock when we reached the floor of the Valley. From there we traveled up the Valley and reached the Yosemite Village about two o'clock, and went to the Ranger's Headquarters and asked for a camp. He asked me if I had ever been here before and I answered 'Yes.' He asked me what camp I wanted. 'Camp Seven' was my reply. We went up to Camp Seven, but it was so closely crowded with campers that we kept on going up the Merced River until we came to Camp Fourteen,[1] a camp with only a few campers and a very fine meadow in back. It is along the river just opposite Royal Arches."

After two days of rest, the brothers began training their mounts for the traditional Fourth of July races. Strent had ridden Victorina, "our fastest horse, into the Valley to get her into these races. John rode Buck, a spunky little Indian pony who is always ready to race.

---

1. Camp 7 is now called Lower River, and Camp 14 is Lower Pines.

Strentzel Hanna won second prize, $15.00, in the Free-for-All race. Here spectators urged him on as he won the second heat. (Jim Hanna Collection)

"On the Fourth, the first thing on the program was the potato race. The two sides, of six each, were the 'Rangers' against the 'Guides.' The next thing that furnished a good time was the Tug of War which lasted about ten minutes. The sides were the 'Rangers' against the 'Guides' and the 'Packers.' The men rode bareback and had cow horses who were trained to go forward or backward moving only an inch or so at a time. The 'Guides' and 'Packers' pulled hard at first, but at the end the 'Rangers' gave one hard pull and won by a foot or so.

"These two main events took place in front of Camp Yosemite while the main events were to take place in the meadow below the Village. Soon all of the machines started up and everybody tried to get there first."

Just west of the Village a grandstand had been erected and decorated. Judges, local dignitaries, and the "orator of the Day" sat there. "All the motorists parked their cars along the road and crowded up to the grandstand." After the speeches, foot races for men and boys took place, followed by the main event—the horse races. Indians from as far away as Mono Lake entered the Indian pony race.

"John entered our pony Buck, who is a real Indian pony from the Navajo Indian Reservation in Arizona, in this race, but the distance was too long for her so John only came in third and did not win any money for there were only two prizes. John was the only rider in this race who was not an Indian, but he argued so well that it was a race for Indian ponies, which Buck was, that the judges let him ride, which made some of the Indians angry."

Strent had entered Victorina in the Free-for-All race. Indians, cowboys, and the Hanna boys made twelve starters divided into two heats, since the road, doubling as race track, was too narrow for more than six mounts at a time. Strent came in first in the second heat, John third in the first heat. Later the winners of both heats competed. The spectators shouts "could be heard over a mile," Strent said, and "people crowded over and under the ropes," and "some stood on top of their automobiles so they could see." A sorrel mare beat Victorina, but Strent pocketed fifteen dollars for second prize. François Matthes wrote in his diary for July 4: "Went to Yosemite Valley in the morning and witnessed the races and other events to celebrate the Fourth of July. In the pony races two boys distinguished themselves—both [of them] grandsons of John Muir."

"After the races we stayed in the Valley about a week to buy a few supplies and then went out for it was getting hot and there was no fishing. We went up Tenaya Canyon past Mirror Lake to a point opposite Half Dome to ascend its [the canyon's] side. Tenaya Canyon is a deep canyon scoured out of solid rock by large glaciers and only a few men have ever gone up its entire length. It is solid granite highly polished by the ice. The trail up the side is zig-zag and in places there were 25 or more in succession, every turn about four feet apart. The three horses we had were often 10 or 15 feet above each other. The first rider could often meet the last one face to face near enough to talk to him.

"This is the Snow Creek Trail and the only fault with it is that it is hot and dusty."

That night they camped at Tenaya Lake. "In the morning we started for the Tuolumne Meadows about 8 miles from here which I think are the finest meadows in the Sierra. Through the Meadows flows the Tuolumne River, one of the coldest in the mountains, for its two upper forks come from the Dana and Lyell Glaciers, the latter being the largest glacier in the Sierra."

A half century earlier, John Muir, on his first exposure to what he termed the "flowery lawns" of Tuolumne Meadows, had described it as "the most spacious and delightful pleasure-ground I have yet seen." As had their grandfather, Strent and John made a central camp from "where we could go on all the one day trips we wanted."

Dog Lake, beyond Lembert Dome, was their first destination. Strent's comment on the trip was surprisingly mature. "Many people hurry up and try to break a record for fast climbing, but before they get half way they quit and stay there an hour or so and sometimes they go back. But if a person goes up slow and admires God's work as he goes he will often get there before the fellow who tried to get there first.

"Some people think that Dog Lake has the shape of a dog but this is not true. It has an oblong shape with two small bays at the lower end. There is a sand-bar in the lake that does not come out of the water but in places is only three or four feet from the surface but in other places the lake is so deep and the water so clear that it is a dark blue color almost black."[2]

Strent's favorite pastime was fishing. "Of all the streams and creeks I have ever fished in, I like Delaney Creek the best. Delaney Creek is not very large and at nearly any place a good jumper can jump clear across it but I do not advise anyone to try it for it is a narrow gorge from five to ten feet wide and twenty feet deep. About every quarter of a mile there are waterfalls or cascades and at the bottom of these there are always plenty of fish.

"But the fisherman must hide behind a rock or lie down on the bank, for if the fish get one glimpse of him or his rod they hide behind or under a rock.

"One day I came to camp with a nice string of fish, A fellow camped above us asked me where

---

2. Robert B. Marshall of the U.S. Geological Survey named the lake in 1898 when he found an abandoned sheepdog and her litter of puppies there. (*Yosemite Place Names*, p. 35.)

I caught them. I told him in Delaney Creek and he asked me if I would go with him. This man was a tenderfoot who had never fished for trout. I taught him how to cast his line and told him what flies or bait was best to use for the different kind of water we would fish in.

"In this meadow there is more sunlight than there is on the pools in the creek so when I came here I had to change my fly."

Delaney Creek was named for Pat Delaney, the sheep-owner who had hired Muir to accompany his 2,000-plus sheep and a herder that memorable and fateful summer of 1869. In hiring Muir, Delaney inadvertently gave him the goal of ridding the high country of "hoofed locusts," and the desire to explore and understand the glaciers that had created the meadows, gouged out the canyons, and rounded the domes of the Yosemite region. Strent must have known those things, but did not allude to them. In fact, nowhere in his trip account did Strent mention his illustrious grandfather. Both the Muir and Hanna names were well-known, however, and people who recognized the relationship were no doubt impressed with the independence of the young boys, and treated them with unusual attention.

"While we were in the Tuolumne Meadows, Mr. [Stephen] Mather, the director of all the National Parks in the United States was camped there with his party. One day they decided to go to Elizabeth Lake for a picnic and asked me to go along. Some rode horseback and some walked.

"I offered two of the boys that were going to walk a ride for we had three horses and we always had to let them all go for none would stay alone. They said they had ridden before and helped me catch the horses, for we always turned them loose. If they had ever ridden before they must have ridden plugs for one of the boys got on, and right off when the horse started and the other boy only rode as far as our camp when he had ridden far enough.

"We all had light lunches,", Strent added, "which were not heavy enough for we were all very hungry.

"At the same time we were in the Meadows, an immense party of campers, members of the Sierra Club, camped on their property, a quarter section of land near Lembert's Dome." Grandfather Muir

had been a moving spirit behind the Sierra Club's founding in 1892, as well as its president until his death. Muir's close friend and successor as the Club's president, Will Colby, was in charge of the 1919 two-week outing. Undoubtedly it was he who invited the boys to join the 175 members. No matter how self-reliant they were, Strent and John must have enjoyed the congenial company, the attention, and the meals, prepared by Chinese chefs—though not necessarily in that order.

In 1915 the Club had built what Strent described as "a beautiful granite lodge, with stone from the mountain just behind." Named for a recently deceased Club director, Parsons Memorial Lodge was one huge room with an enormous fireplace and stone and slab benches. "One day a severe rain and thunder storm came up and everybody began 'to pack up their troubles in their old kit bag' and seek the Lodge for shelter. Soon everyone with kit and sleeping bag was inside. The rain turned into hail, the worst hail storm I ever saw. The log rafters of the Lodge have a tin roof. Inside one could not hear thunder when the hail was beating down.

"That night many slept in the Lodge. The hail stopped, then it rained. After the evening talks, the log benches were rolled along the middle. The men slept on one side while the women used the other.

"The floor was made of gravel scattered over the earth and granite. At first it felt pretty good but soon rocks of all sizes worked their way up. A steady groan from the sleepers could be heard all night. I had at least twenty good sized rocks in my bed for feathers. John and a few others who were lucky enough to sleep by the fireplace enjoyed a good night's rest. In the morning everybody was up and dressed long before daylight. Several got up about midnight and played poker until morning."

One night Mather addressed the assemblage on the need for preservation of redwoods in Humboldt County. On July 25, Will Colby led about half the members on a two-day excursion to Mt. Conness. John and Strent left their horses behind, and hadn't walked 150 yards before Strent "picked up an 'Indian Arrow-head' . . . almost a perfect specimen, an inch and a half long, half an inch wide and tapered to a very

Parsons Lodge was, and is, a handsome building, but its then gravel floor made a miserable place to sleep. (Courtesy, The Bancroft Library)

sharp point." Because the Chinese cooks hadn't arrived at the night's camp on the largest of the Young Lakes, the multi-talented Colby acted as cook. The campfire speaker that night was François Matthes "of the United States Geological Survey [who] gave a very interesting lecture on the geology of the surrounding cliffs, mountains and streams."

The ascent of Mt. Conness was made before lunchtime on July 26. "The view from this mountain I shall always remember," Strent enthused. "From the top [altitude 12,590 feet] I saw three glaciers, one was almost directly below me, at least twenty beautiful mountain lakes including Tenaya Lake, all of the domes around Yosemite Valley and the summit peaks for miles around."

On August 2, a week after the Sierra Clubbers, the boys broke camp because "our 'jerky' was gone and all our supplies were running low." That afternoon at Tenaya Lake, two of the Club's

packers stopped and said that all they had eaten for three days was "hardtack and cheese." "We gave them a hot dinner consisting of a pot of chocolate, eighteen big trout which we had brought from Tuolumne Meadows and all the hot cakes and biscuits they could eat.

"During the night mountain lions screamed and scared our horses so badly they ran away. The ground here was soft and two of our horses were hobbled. When the hobbled horses ran, their feet came down together and made tracks that were easy to follow."

Nonetheless, John couldn't locate them before breakfast, and afterward the boys followed tracks "about two miles where we found the horses in a narrow canyon so steep at the upper end that they could not go any farther."

Just before they reached Tenaya Lake, Bethel had lost a shoe. Victorina had a loose shoe and all of Buck's needed attention, so Strent unpacked his tools, "put a nail in one of Victorina's shoes and tightened and clinched the rest. This was easy. Bethel's foot was badly torn so I had to cut down her hoof with the rasp and butcher knife. Bethel is only a colt and would not stand still, when we tried to pick up her foot she would kick at us but she never hit either of us.

"When I had the hoof smooth and level I fitted the shoe all around and nailed it on. A good blacksmith will make the points of the eight nails come out of the shoe in a level line about an inch and a half above the shoe. All of my nails came out, but very irregularly. It took me about two hours to put on one shoe while a blacksmith can put on four in one hour."

The next morning they left the lake, traveled west "a couple of miles over bare granite where we saw many ground hogs [marmots]. In the afternoon we traveled some more fine timber, past Snow Creek to the rim of Yosemite Valley where the zig zags begin. It was extra hot going down them for it was late in the day and the trail was very dusty."

By that time, mid-August, most of the snow-fed waterfalls were dry, and the floor of Yosemite Valley dry, hot, and dusty, but "we camped on the bank of Tenaya Creek near a meadow with good grass in it." From there, Strent said, "We made a few trips to the places where tourists usually go." He described only one of these, a trip to Glacier Point by the Four-Mile Trail and back via the 'Eleven-Mile Trail.' At that time, the former trail ascended over 3,000 feet in three miles. "It is so steep," Strent wrote, "that it is full of zigs and zags but it is cool and shady in the morning.

"At the end of two miles we came to a pine tree that had been struck by lightning. On the snag there was a sign, 'HALFWAY TREE.' Further on we crossed an ice cold stream where we drank nearly as much water as our horses did.

Sierra Club party at the summit of Mount Conness on July 26, 1919. In his diary, François Matthes wrote: "Reached the top in comfort 11 a.m. Stayed there until 1 p.m. with Mr. Forsyth and Strentzel Hanna." (Photo by Russell Bacon. Courtesy, The Bancroft Library)

On July 24, 1919, Lillian Grosvenor, Gabrielle Sovulewski, Frances Capps, and Donna Solinsky joined the Sierra Club at least long enough to have their picture taken. (Photo by Francis P. Farquhar. Courtesy, The Bancroft Library)

"At Union Point there is a large cigar shaped rock,[3] standing on end and nearby, a deserted ranger cabin. It was a mile from here to Glacier Point and the trail was not steep.

"During the morning we passed many people who were walking. The trail was steep, and the people were not used to walking so could only go a little way and then stop to take a rest. So many stopped that there was a regular line of tired people along the trail. Many took hold of our horses' tails and got a lift."

Atop Glacier Point, Strent was annoyed because stablemen working for the Yosemite National Park Company refused to sell them hay for their horses, and he was put off by the high charges at the cafeteria, housed in McCauley's former Mountain House. "We got a good meal, but not as much to eat as we got at Camp Curry." Just south of the lunchroom was the big Glacier Point Hotel, which had opened in 1917.[4] "The hotel is new and

---

3. Agassiz Column.

4. Both the Mountain House and the Glacier Point Hotel were destroyed by fire in August 1969.

Agassiz Column was a landmark on the pioneer route of the Four-Mile Trail. (YRL Collection)

has a veranda twelve feet wide and one hundred feet long across the front. From here we saw the peaks around Tuolumne Meadows which looked like sharp rocks sticking up into the sky while the nearer peaks looked larger. Half Dome looked as if we could jump onto it but it was over a mile away.

"There were many fine maps and a model of Yosemite Valley on the veranda." Far below the point itself, "the Merced River looked like a great snake crawling the valley and automobiles themselves looked like ants traveling on their trails.

People swimming in the tank at Camp Curry looked like minnows in a pool."

Returning to the Valley via Panorama Cliff on the 'Eleven-Mile Trail' took the boys through "fine forests," past Illilouette, Nevada, and Vernal falls, and finally above the Merced River's boisterous white water. "We listened to the roar of the river and admired the beautiful pools and cascades all the way down to the valley," Strent wrote.

As August neared its end the boys packed up for home, going out via the precipitous, zig-zagging controlled section of the Big Oak Flat Road. "The road is so steep and narrow that it is hard for an automobile to even pass a saddle horse so the Park Rangers make all the automobiles leaving the Valley go up for one hour, the next hour the automobiles entering the Valley can come down. We were not yet to the top when the machines began to come down. It was not so steep here and we were able to ride our horses above the road."

That night the boys camped near a "little wet meadow," and the next day they traveled through "fine timber," including the sequoias in the Tuolumne Grove of Big Trees. "Everybody that ever sees these trees is satisfied with their size. Some things are given too much credit for their size and beauty but these trees cannot be given a good enough description." John Muir said that sequoias were "the king of all conifers, not only in size but in sublime majesty."

By evening the boys reached Crocker's Station, where Muir had often stayed or picked up mail and supplies. "The hotel was closed," Strent wrote, "and the owner was packing up his furniture. Right behind the hotel there was a fine meadow with a good fence all around it where we camped.

"We got an early start in the morning for we did not have to lose any time hunting for our horses. It was the first time during our trip that they were inside a fence and couldn't wander away. Here we left the real mountains, or God's country, the timber began to get smaller and to grow more scatteringly and up to noon we crossed only two small streams."

Four days later, after a hot and uncomfortable night atop sacks of grain and potatoes on the boat from Stockton to Crockett, John and Strent "got off the boat, and it was just daylight, August 29, 1919, when we got home."

Reticent to the end, Strent did not elaborate on what must have been a joyous family reunion, or mention their parents' welcome to the sun-tanned tatterdemalions who surely had grown physically and emotionally during their wonderful summer in the Sierra.

8

The 1920s

YOSEMITE did not truly join the modern world until July 31, 1926, when the All-Year Highway—state route 140—winding up the Merced River Canyon, was finally opened. At that time, roads, bridges, trails, and campgrounds throughout Yosemite needed either improvement or replacement. There were no paved roads, no modern hotel, and no adequate hospital or sanitation systems in the Park. Housing for Park Service and concessionaire staffs was sorely needed.

The completion of the road had an immediate and beneficial affect on the residents of Yosemite and El Portal. Until then, all high school age children had to attend schools in Fresno or in some more distant place, where they boarded with friends or relatives. The bus ride to Mariposa High—over an hour each way—was trying, and after-hours activities impossible except for those who boarded in Mariposa during the week, but the families were no longer disrupted by the prolonged absences of their teenagers.

In many ways the earlier 1924–25 period was crucial for cohesive development in Yosemite Valley. A planned community and government

Government Center, renamed Yosemite Village, was carefully planned by Park Service engineers. Most of the buildings in this 1927 photograph still exist, but the ugly parking area is now an attractive mall. (YRL Collection)

center, designed by Park Service engineers and funded in large part by Congress, was begun on the sunny north side of the Valley to replace the incongruous collection of structures crowded into Old Village. Two large rustic-style buildings of wood and stone, to house the Park Service headquarters and a Park Museum, were built at the western end of the new complex. A post office and Foley's Studio were placed at the eastern end of this arc of buildings. Immediately west of the post office, Pillsbury's, Best's, and Boysen's were assigned sites for their new shops. Living quarters were to be built back of them.

When questioned as to whether hostility had been manifested by any of the concessionaires to these moves, Virginia Best replied, "I didn't hear any resentment. I know [Arthur] Pillsbury was the first to want to move. He was always keen at taking on new things. We just *did* what the government wanted us to do, at our own expense of course.

"We were assigned a place, a site, and we had to make buildings fit in. Actually we were on a glacial moraine that was full of rocks. Dad got tired of trying to move all those rocks and built the back part several feet higher than the front."

Pillsbury was indeed the first to adapt. His new building, opened in 1924, was large, handsome, and in harmony with the landscape. "The new studio was wonderful," nephew Art thought, "and in back there was a regular movie theater where commercial movies were shown three nights a week. There were regular movie projectors, and a typical player-piano combo on which a woman played . . . drums and musical instruments were part of it." She accompanied the silent films of the day.

Beyond that structure, which included a storage room and darkrooms, "was room for parking cars, and up against the rocks there were cottages for Uncle and Aunt Aetheline and the manager of the studio. I stayed in a tent with a floor, around a rock." Art's main job during college vacations was operating the movie projectors, "and I did most of the kodak finishing."

Barely three years later, a fire burned the theater, projection room, darkrooms, "all of Uncle's negatives, his stock of pictures . . . equipment . . . most of his own inventive projects, were gone."

Only the front part of the studio survived.

Pillsbury was devastated. He sold out to the Yosemite Park and Curry Company, and left Yosemite, but continued activities in photography and on lecture tours elsewhere. Today, a flattish granite rock, west of the Ansel Adams Gallery—formerly Best's Studio—inscribed "Pillsbury's Pictures 1924" remains, as do many of his photographs and thousands of postcards. These collector's images memorialize this talented and remarkable man. Until their deaths, Ernest, Grace, and Art retained their love of Yosemite and pride in their Uncle.

It was 1926 before Harry Best's simple, attractive new quarters opened with its darkrooms, employee cottages, and his home behind it. Soon after settling in what initially was called Government Center and later became the Village, Virginia said, "We could hear Indian dancing going on to the east. Dad, the young woman who worked for us, and I walked up to the Indian Village, where the hospital was built later. When they saw Dad, an Indian called, 'Hi, Best, come on! Come and dance!' He did a little and we girls saw the Indians as if we had never seen them before.

"They danced around, and there was an old, old man, I think from the Tuolumne River side, who was evidently coaching them on dancing. That was interesting."

By that time, Chris Brown, named for artist Chris Jorgensen for whom his pretty mother Lena worked, had transformed himself into "Chief Lemee," meaning "ripple on the water." As a boy, he had learned the dances, chants, and rituals of his ancestors, but had no particular status in the dwindling Native American population.

When questioned about Chris, whom she had known since childhood, Virginia said, "He made himself a chief! He just acquired that title. Sometime in the early twenties he went off with Herbert Earl Wilson [an entertainer at Camp Curry and author of a slim book on Indian lore] to the Southwest. There he saw how effective the Indians were with feathers in their hair and things like that. When he came back, he had all sorts of ideas, which he developed."

As Chief Lemee—in war paint, headdress, beadwork, and feathered costume, accompanied

The long and the short of it: Beatrice Murphy, Ruth Jewett, Billy McPeak, Edna Jewett, unidentified lad, Joe Jobe, and trouble-prone Jack Muldoon. (Ruth Jewett Metzler Collection)

by guttural chants—he worked part-time for the evolving Park naturalist division. Strict authenticity was secondary to entertainment, until later. Lemee thrilled audiences, especially children, with his spirited dances.

In connection with the 1926 opening of the All-Year Highway, the Park Service sponsored a seventy-fifth anniversary of the Mariposa Battalion's discovery of Yosemite. Ironically, descendants of the Native Americans, whose life style was ended by the civilian soldiers, were asked to participate in the celebration! The man who won the prize for being the best dressed Indian was a white man named Edwin Jones! Each summer he, his wife, and daughter Dorothy camped for weeks in the Valley. She was twelve

that year, and still remembers the festivities.

"Somehow my dad, a doctor in the Bay Area, became friendly with the Indians, and they talked him into dressing up as an Indian. After the parade there was a 'field day' held at Royal Arch Meadow. One of the events was the Indian [Edwin Jones] shooting a bow and arrow against the white man [Herbert Earl Wilson]. A stuffed crane was brought from the museum, and the 'Indian' shot the neck off the crane—much to my dad's surprise.

"I remember after the pageant we found a picture of my dad with Lemee, Bill Tad from Mono Lake, and Chief Ranger Townsley for sale in one of the shops in the new village." A few years later, "The Indians honored Dad by adopting him into

Ranger Bert Sault and his son Bill lived in this small house in about 1926. It was a recycled prefabricated cabin first used for employee housing on the Owens Valley Aqueduct project. Even in 1993, several units are still used in Yosemite Valley, where they are known as WOBS—rooms without baths. (William E. Sault Collection)

even though their second bedrooms were not much bigger than closets.

"We were the first to move in," wrote Ken Carpenter, son of maintenance department manager E. T. "Carp" Carpenter. "There I spent the years until I graduated from Mariposa High School in 1934." Among his playmates were Bobby and Billy Lintott, who lived next door. Their mother, Rose, "played a loud honky-tonk piano and was the featured performer at all the parties and dances at the [Old Village] Pavilion."

"We were a close-knit group of families," Ken commented. "In the evenings the parents would sit in the front yards and watch us play: Pom-Pom-Pullaway, Statues, King of the Hill, One-O-Cat, and other games. Every fall the meadow would be mowed by horse-drawn mowers and [the grass] raked into piles. Jumping into these was irresistible, despite the scolding we would get for scattering the hay."

In 1927 the Knowles family moved into the rock fabric house, the only one with a fireplace. After the new family arrived, the rock house had another distinction: it was the only one to boast a Chinese houseboy.[1]

"Knowles was neither Company nor Government," Ken wrote, "but an independent contractor having the Standard Oil contract to deliver gasoline and other Standard products to the Valley. Mrs. Knowles (I think it was) was independently wealthy—thus the houseboy."

Before Knowles took the contract a man named Art Wilkinson had charge of the Standard Oil station next to the garage. No rock houses for him— just a tent in the summer, and two tents during the one winter he and his family stayed in the Valley. Sons Bob and Clayton attended Yosemite

the tribe. Chief Lemee put on a ceremony by the pool at the foot of Yosemite Falls during a full moon. There was lots of chanting and dancing. Dad was given an Indian headdress and named Tno Yuk Wiyaka, meaning doctor of Indians."

Despite the moves, Old Village was far from deserted, for there still were Degnan's, the general store, the Pavilion—where movies were shown—the deteriorating Sentinel Hotel group, Park Service and Curry Company offices, plus many employee cottages. It was not until 1959 that the last old structure, the Village Store, was demolished, because a new one on the north side of the Valley had finally replaced it.

Coinciding with the Park Service building boom, which included a housing complex northeast of the new center, the Curry Company and former Desmond interests merged, became the Yosemite Park and Curry Company, and accelerated construction of staff housing. Six small houses with identical interiors, but differing exteriors—wood, stucco, stone, hollow tile, and even a type of metal—all facing Ahwahnee Meadow, were completed in 1924. Dubbed "The Row," these places were for staff with families,

---

1. Later, Lee Hung, renamed Homer Lee, became a well-known florist in Berkeley

Elementary School.

School was okay, but it was a lot more fun to attend a party honoring screen star Clara Bow. No other children were present, and the boys danced the Charleston before an audience of more than eighty adults.

Another of Bob's vivid memories was of standing in front of an airplane that had landed below Old Village in the early twenties. It wasn't the first one to land—that had occurred in 1919—but might have been one of the last, since the Park Service banned planes from landing in the narrow valley. At Wawona, however, a 3,000-foot airstrip was laid out in the long, privately-owned Wawona Meadow about 1924. Until fencing was built, it was tomboy Wawona Washburn's job to leap on her horse, often bareback, race down to the airstrip, and chase away the hotel's dairy herd so that an airplane could land.[2]

Although Yosemite Valley was geographically isolated, films, radio, and the All-Year Highway decreased its communication and transportation deficiencies. Statistics dramatically document the change. In 1925, 209,000 people visited the Park. That jumped to 274,000 in 1926, and to a staggering 490,000 in 1927, the first full year of travel over the new route.

Not only was Yosemite in touch with the world, but the world came to it—some by rail, others by the three roads. Among the proliferating multitudes were VIPs: King Albert of Belgium, the Crown Prince of Sweden, the premier of Greece, Tom Mix, Clara Bow, Will Rogers, Lord and Lady Astor, Herbert Hoover, Mary Roberts Rinehart, Doug Fairbanks, Mary Pickford, and Gertrude Stein.

Young Audrey Beck, whose father specialized in preparing firefalls, remembers the day when her parents took her to the Ahwahnee Hotel for

Before they were prohibited, several airplanes landed safely in Yosemite Valley; the first one was in 1919. This one attracted a marveling group, including Bob and Clayton Wilkinson, in the mid-1920s. The plane was a Standard J-1 with a 150-horsepower Hispano-Suiza engine. (Robert Wilkinson Collection)

a reception honoring Guglielmo Marconi. Few children now would recognize the name Marconi, but then it was almost a household word, since he had won the Nobel Prize for inventing the radio. Marconi graciously shook hands with everyone standing in the reception line. Awed by his achievement and courtly manner, Audrey determined "never to wash my hands again."

Teenager Don Blank and a friend had an even more exciting encounter after hiking the thirteen miles between the Valley and Merced Lake. Although numbers of people were staying at the High Sierra Camp, the boys were the sole occupants of the adjacent campground. As they were about to open a can of beans, Don reminisced, a man strolled over, identified himself as a Secret Service agent, and "asked us if we would like to meet President Hoover who was staying at the camp with friends. Naturally we were honored and lucky to meet the President and he was very gracious and down to earth and even gave us some of the trout he and his friends had caught that day."[3]

Later, Don was to marvel that, except for the Secret Service agents and a rowboat that was packed in for him, the President of the United

---

2. In 1941, nine years after the Washburn family sold their holdings to the Park Service, the dangerous airstrip was eliminated, and the meadow allowed to return to nature.

3. So avid a fisherman and Yosemite devotee was Hoover that Chief Ranger Forest Townsley, a fishing companion of the president, in the late 1920s named three small lakes and a creek—north of Buena Vista Crest—for Hoover.

Bob and Clayton Wilkinson's father, Art, had the Standard Oil contract in the mid 1920s. (Bob Wilkinson Collection)

Glenn and Bob Gallison, were the fourth generation of their family in Yosemite.

In the 1920s, "When Glenn learned to fish and was so intent on it, he barely got home before dark. After this happened a second time, Mom took his pole away for a week and then got him a cheap watch." He never tired of fishing, "but Gallison Lake was named for Dad, Arthur Gallison, because he planted fish in it way back in 1916.

"We three kids went to the Park Service nature school every summer and grew up appreciating the wildlife. Once, while Mom was gone, we coaxed a deer up on our front steps and into the living room with bread as bait. That was dangerous. Another time we helped chase away a bear who was trying to get into the back porch.

"Pets weren't allowed in the Park, but we had mice and squirrels in the walls of our house, and deer wandering across our yard.

"The neighbor kids played Ante-Over with us after supper—over the roof-tops and baseball in the street. Happy memories!"

The Gallisons occupied a new house in the Lost Arrow area where, eventually, all Park Service personnel would live in brown-painted structures. The area was backed by Sunnyside Bench, John Muir's winter haunt, and the Lost Arrow, a tapering rock spear. Until sometime in the early 1960s, the buildings of Soapsuds Row had been converted to Park Service housing, as were a few cottages on the long since closed road to the base of Yosemite Falls.[4] The hospital, built by cavalry troops in 1912, stood east of this road.

Concessionaire housing was grouped between the Ahwahnee meadow and the barn-like Curry auto repair garage, although a few employees

States was traveling by horseback to several of the High Sierra Camps in a fairly normal manner. No helicopter standing by, no media coverage, no black box. "How relatively serene the nation and the world were then despite the stock market crash and impending signs of the Depression."

Fishing was a passion of many Yosemite youths. "Our ice box, and later a refrigerator, always contained fresh-caught trout," recalled Dorothy Gallison (Sprague). She and her brothers,

---

4. Soapsuds Row, originally ten or so army officers' quarters, existed in part until the early 1960s. "The Row," concessionaire housing facing the Ahwahnee meadow, is still in use.

lived in Old Village or at Camp Curry. The houses were universally gray. The Indians occupied the west bank of Indian Creek.

Children mingled at the newest school, a many-windowed, high-roofed building erected in 1916–17 in the Lost Arrow neighborhood. All of them either walked or bicycled the distance to school. The town-gown schism, mentioned earlier by Hart Cook, was probably increased by the geographic segregation that was elaborated upon by Ken Carpenter.

"There was a rigid social fabric to Yosemite. The vertical divisions, of course: Company, Government, independents such as Pillsbury, Best, Boysen, and the Degnans (divided horizontally with the lowest rungs occupied by such people as the barber, the shoemaker, the Swiss woodcutter, etc.), the Dudes, and the Indians.

"Parties were one of the few social outlets in those days. My parents were party givers and party goers. Yet in all the years I lived on the row I cannot remember ever any member of the higher divisions being in the house, or my parents being in theirs. For that matter, cross-cultural mixing was rare between Government and Company."

Mixing was also rare between the Native American and the white children. Ranger's son Bill Sault remembers physical encounters when he was the new kid in school, about 1926. "The Indian kids were tough, but so was I, and we ended up friends. Once I was asked over to their camp."[5]

During the late 1920s, noise from hammers, saws, and heavy equipment often overwhelmed the sounds of Yosemite Falls. Valley children liked to ride bikes to the former site of the stables and watch the massive Ahwahnee Hotel taking shape.

A newspaper reporter lauded fourteen-year-old John Reymann's worm farm as "perhaps the only industry of its kind in the United States if not in the entire world." John posed with a worm in his fingers, and others displayed on a cloth. He charged fishermen a quarter a dozen for his squirming bait, and took in $1.75 in one day in 1927. (John Reymann Collection)

Ranger Bill Reymann's son John vividly recalls the thrill of jumping from high girders onto a stockpile of sand. After the hotel opened, in July 1927, it was fun to watch guest cottages being built on the hotel grounds. Employee housing, including dormitories, was under construction between the Row and the still existing cavernous automobile repair garage. Best of all, a four-track toboggan slide was erected at right angles to Ash Can Alley, near Camp Curry, which provided thrills for residents and guests.

---

5. During the 1920s, at least, only a handful of Indian children attended school in Yosemite. Most of them, particularly those of high school age, were sent to the Stewart Indian School in Nevada.

Marian Starr and Rusty Rust wearing medals they had won for juvenile girls and juvenile boys ice-skating championships in January 1931. (Yosemite Park & Curry Co. Collection. YP & CC)

Creation of the largest outdoor skating rink in the West was an easier accomplishment. Quickly frozen water was repeatedly spread over Camp Curry's parking lot, and the resulting ice made a rink far superior to the natural ones that formed on the Merced River. The river, Mirror Lake, and an abandoned gravel pit froze solid only in extremely cold winters. After the man-made rink opened, in 1928, it was immediately popular with guests and residents, young and old.

The Curry Company's development of winter sports, mainly to attract guests during winters, was a boon to resident children. Eight-year-old Rusty, who had learned to skate on river ice, quickly established himself as the Hans Brinker

of Yosemite, outskating adults as well as children. Rusty was born on Soapsuds Row in April 1920, the son of Jess Rust, a former stagedriver, and Hilda Jeffrey Rust, granddaughter of pioneer Coulterville hotelkeepers.

Inevitably his first volunteer jobs, and later his paid ones, were in the post office. Although he was not an outstanding student at Yosemite Elementary, teachers and students liked his sunny disposition and enthusiasm. He excelled almost from the first, however, on ice. When he was eight, the huge outdoor rink, in the shadow of Half Dome, opened at Camp Curry. It channeled his energies, and inspired in him the ambition to be the best. To finance his many hours on the ice, he hauled empty toboggans up the steep hill to the top of the track—at two bits a haul. Even when winded, he relished the view of Half Dome

Maybe it was "Old Mokus" who chased John Reymann and Jack Muldoon up a tree. (Shirley Sault Randolph Collection)

64

from the summit.

Four years later, Rusty won the first of numerous local and state championships in speed, figure, and pairs skating, with Catherine Lally as his partner in the pairs. His skill and trophy increased, but not his ego.

"Soon after my dad became Yosemite's chief naturalist," Everett Harwell testified, "I found myself matched—mismatched, actually—with Rusty in a race. True, I was eleven, and Rusty was younger, but he was born with silver skates. I must have been a sight—in knickers, knee-length stockings, and a heavy, new sheepskin coat, making my way around the rink with ankles at awkward angles, arms flailing, and inevitably falling flat.

"Rusty, the good sport, would help me up, hold me up, and lead me by the hand, sometimes while he was skating backward!

"And so, of course, he won, but he was the only person who ever beat me in a race—for the simple reason that I never again raced anyone on ice skates!"

Ice skating was *the* nighttime winter entertainment between 1923 and 1940. Bear feeding was the popular nighttime spectator "sport" for residents and visitors during summers. It began, innocently enough, even earlier, when hotel owners got rid of their garbage by providing a feast for the bears and pleasure for people. Later, nocturnal raids in campgrounds were averted, or at least lessened, since bears congregated at a feeding site a mile west of Old Village. There the river separated viewers from eaters, floodlights illuminated the bears, and a ranger-naturalist provided an interpretive program, trying to explain the unnatural, circus-like scene. Children loved it, probably no one more than Betty Haigh, who says now, "Bear feeding? Why, that was the social event of the day! Everybody went! As soon as the men dumped the big cans of garbage, the bears showed up, some of them growling, and the lights came on and the bears began rooting in the mess. And people, tourists and rangers,

School was out, and the elk were being loaded up to leave the Valley in October 1933 when Ralph Anderson took this photograph. (Bob Gallison Collection)

Before the toboggan slide and the skating rink were installed, winter sports such as snowshoeing—or attampts at it—took place in the meadow below the Chapel. (YP & CC Collection)

everybody talked to each other."

Another zoo-like atmosphere, begun innocently to protect wild animals from extinction, was the introduction of twelve Tule elk into Yosemite Valley in 1920. Because this endangered species endangered tourists and their automobiles, they had to be tightly fenced in the twenty-eight-acre meadow between the Ahwahnee Hotel and the northeast corner of Sentinel Bridge. During the next thirteen years, before the herd was relocated to Owens Valley, the grass in the meadow was nearly obliterated, and the elk population more than doubled.

At first, Yosemite youngsters were fascinated by the exotic but surly animals, but soon their interest waned. John Reymann and his equally trouble-prone sidekick, Jack Muldoon, were exceptions. They coveted sets of antlers which, they noted, were often buried in the dirt by elk after being shed. One afternoon, the teenagers opened

the gate and, after refastening it, cautiously began looking for antlers. "We found some, they were great prizes," John Reymann recounted decades later. "We kept an eye on an old bull who was watching us. He'd eat a little bit, then kinda move toward us. We were pretty careful and had an eye on a thicket of big azaleas and a couple of pine trees just in case. Well, we loaded up when BOOM, man, that bull took after us. I mean he was charging, but then so were we. We dropped those horns, burst through the azaleas and skinned up a tree out of his reach.

"And boy, he was ready to eat us alive, banging into that tree. He just wouldn't go away. We couldn't get down, it's getting kinda dark, so we started hollering and this man heard us from the road. Everybody knows everybody then so he telephoned my dad who said, as he always did, "What's John done now?"

"Dad almost had to hit that bull with his

66

Model T pickup before we could climb down and into the truck. We never got any antlers, though. That was the worst of it."

Although three generations of Curry children "grew up" during summers at Camp Curry, they weren't assimilated into the Yosemite community—partly because of the isolated site near the base of Glacier Point. When Jennie and David Curry, the tireless proprietors of the innovative camp, arrived there in 1899, Foster was eleven, Mary six, and Marjorie four. Their parents were too busy to supervise them, so their grandparents did, but they were free to roam the camp. Foster reveled in fishing, carrying wood, running errands for guests, and emulating his stentorian father in shouting, "ALL'S WELL" or "FAREWELL" to guests. His younger sister Mary was much quieter, shyer, and reflective. Since "I was a child of five when we first came into the Valley," she wrote years later, "my recollections of those first days are necessarily rather limited and chaotic. I remember the wild ride down the old Coulterville Road with Driver Eddie Webb on our first trip in, and I remember how the 4-horse stages used to wheel into the turn-around at the front, with a crack of the driver's whip out of a cloud of dust. My father and a porter or two and any guests who had not gone for hikes or rides would be assembled for the big event of the day, and there would be a warm welcome for the travelers, with much flourishing of feather dusters. Ladies had their hats tied down with heavy veils, and unfortunate was he or she who didn't sport a linen dust-coat. Even in 1915 there was only one mile of hard-paved road in the Valley.

"There were still a number of Indians living in Yosemite part of the year. I remember particularly a couple of the women, Mary, and Lucy who used to take my sister and me to pick wild strawberries in the meadows. They were plentiful in those days, and the women used to bring heaping cans of them to camp and sell them for 'wild strawberry sundaes.' Sometimes, too, 'Cap'n Sam' or

Della Dondero was dressed in her best, and her infant brother John was ensconsed in a cradle basket, when this picture was taken about 1930. (John Reymann Collection)

'Cap'n Tom' would come from the high country or across the crest from Mono through Bloody Canyon with trout in willow creels, packed with ferns and almost icy cold, which at that time they were allowed to sell to us."

All three children started working at the camp as youngsters, thus continuing their segregation from Valley society. After her marriage to Don Tresidder, in 1920, both Mary and Don were closely involved in all community affairs—Don until his death in 1948, and Mary until she died in her top-floor Ahwahnee Hotel suite in 1970.

Marjorie's children, Marjorie Jane and Bobby, as well as their cousin Stuart Cross, spent the long summers at Camp Curry in the 1920s and '30s. While they were small children they attended the Kiddie Kamp, with the wonderful train that encircled it, under the fond eye of its manager, Emily Lane. She referred to the trio as "white elephants" because, Stuart explained, "We did not pay the small daily fee." Furthermore, he said that the "white elephants" were not the only children who lived in Camp Curry because of parental employment. Nell and Roger Lane's mother, Mrs. Emily Lane, was a faithful Curry old-timer, having begun work there in 1912. Natalie Lasky's father was the Camp's candy maker, and Ramses Edris and his sister added color because they were Egyptian; their father was the food and beverage manager.

Because Stuart's grandfather, Rufus Green, and Marjorie and Bobby's parents, for whom they were named, were in top management positions, they were 'special' kids. Stuart recalled that their privileged status was brought home to them at an early age.

"One of our best times was when Bobby Williams found that he could charge items at the Soda Fountain, and for several days took us all there in the afternoon and treated us to ice cream cones. Unfortunately, this somehow came to his grandmother's notice, and to our great regret she cut off his credit. This also led, in

Children loved the Kiddie Kamp and the train at Camp Curry, and their parents delighted in being freed of responsibility. (YP & CC Collection)

68

our house, to some stern lectures concerning the abuse of power.

"Other memories," he added, "are generally benign. Picnics by the river, evening excursions to see the lunar rainbow on Lower Yosemite Falls during the full moon, walks after dinner to watch the evening primroses bloom, the annual 4th of July baseball games, children's riding lessons, and Jim Barnett giving our assigned horses fearsome and romantic names."

The trio never tired of the entertainment and the entertainers at Camp Curry. Glenn Hood's singing, Mrs. Jilson's laugh-producing recitations, Herbert Earl Wilson and Don Tresidder telling Indian stories. Lucy Telles making baskets, as well as Herbert Sonn, the bird man, who employed Stuart one summer as a helper, "wrapping and boxing his popular pine cone creations and teaching me about the blue jays he had tamed.

"The Firefall loomed large," particularly the special occasional firefalls on the 4th of July from Half Dome (not very spectacular) and double falls from Glacier Point.

"We also took advantage of the Park Service's naturalist programs, and I went on many walks led by Charlie and Enid Michael, Dr. Bryant, who talked about the "great chain of being"—Huxley's phrase—that introduced me to the basic concept of ecology at a young age, and Bert Harwell, who amazed us with his ability to whistle bird calls, and made us uneasy with his criticisms of the company."

When he was an adult, Stuart served the Yosemite Park and Curry Company as an executive. After Don's death, Mary became president of the Yosemite Park and Curry Company. Her ashes and, much earlier, Foster's, were scattered in Yosemite. Only Marjorie lived and died far from her childhood haunts. Foster's two sons and a daughter were also active workers during the 1930s. Even though the Curry dynasty ended in 1970, there were three successive owners who retained the distinctive, traditional name of The Yosemite Park and Curry Company until 1993— only six years before the centennial of Camp Curry.[6]

While children grew up in Yosemite, so did the Park Service grope its way via some dubious practices, such as the bear feeding and the unnatural, unsightly zoos, toward a balanced approach to two often conflicting demands: To protect the unique region and at the same time administer it so that Yosemite's owners, the public, could enjoy the Park on good roads, bridges, and trails, and stay in well-regulated campgrounds or hotels with appropriate services and sanitation.

Phyllis Freeland's earliest memories of Yosemite, where she was brought by her mother and ranger father as an infant, have nothing to do with the place's lacks, but everything to do with its lure.

As a young child, she recalled, "I am sitting on my grandmother's lap at Camp Curry. It is dark, and I'm sleepy. I hear a man call out loudly, then a faraway voice answer him. My grandmother softly tells me to look up, and I see a 'waterfall' of glowing pink and orange coals spill down the cliff. I watch in a spell.

"Sometimes my mother sings to me when it's time to go to sleep. But when she leaves me, another loved voice is there with me, hushing me to sleep; the voice all Yosemite babies remember, of Yosemite Falls.

"I'm sitting in the back seat of the Ford beside baby brother's basket, my father driving and my mother crying, as we leave the Valley forever for a life in other National Parks."

"Forever" lasted only until Phyllis was old enough to work in Yosemite, and later to live there with her ranger husband Rod Broyles, and another generation of children to be lulled to sleep by Yosemite Falls.

6. In October 1993 a new concessionaire will take over ownership and control. By Park Service edict, the Curry name will be eliminated, except at Curry Village—the present name for Camp Curry.

9

A Decade of Changes

A LTHOUGH the 1920s had been a decade of enormous changes for Yosemite, especially in transportation and communication, there were many other noteworthy developments in the 1930s. A lot of them were caused by the nation-wide Great Depression and the governmental actions to combat it. Three of the so-called alphabet agencies created by President Franklin D. Roosevelt and Congress to put people back to work affected the Park. They were the Civilian Conservation Corps (CCC, or the three C's), the already-established Bureau of Public Roads (BPR), and the Works Progress Administration (WPA).

During those ten years, the Wawona Road and the mile-long Wawona Tunnel were completed, and the new Tioga and Big Oak Flat roads were roughly ninety percent complete. All three highways were built by private contracting firms under the strict supervision and engineering of the BPR. The biggest event of the decade was the inclusion of the Wawona Basin into Yosemite National Park. Another significant acquisition was that of 15,570 acres of largely sugar pine forest on the northwest boundary of the Park. Among the new buildings constructed were the Big Tree Lodge, the Mariposa Grove Museum,

By December 1933, Yosemite's Indian residents were settled in the new village. From left to right: Hazel Oliver holding Jackie Oliver, Amy Hilliard, Agnes Castro, Hazel Warren, Virginia Parker holding her son Ralph, various Beale, Castro, and Parker children, and Velda Johnson on the end. The men in the back are: Al Rhoan, Pete Hilliard, George Warren, and Nelson Oliver. The woman is Irene Beale, holding her child's hand. (YRL Collection)

Mobility was all-important to Jay Johnson, pushing Joe Rhoan in a wheelbarrow while Evelyn Brocchini watched, Carl Dondero pushing Burleigh Johnson in a wagon, Beatrice Rhoan, Charlie Castro, Barbara Bertocini, Patricia Castro, and Beverly Rust. (YRL Collection)

new entrance stations, public rest rooms, numerous residences, a ski lodge at Badger Pass, and a new Indian Village. The first five CCC camps were set up in 1933, and in December 1937 a disastrous flood inundated Yosemite Valley.

Yosemite's children were spectators, if not participants, in most of these milestone events, and some of their memories enliven this chapter.

Not all of the changes were universally welcomed. Residents agreed that a modern hospital was needed, but the sixty-seven surviving Native Americans objected because the site chosen by the Park Service, between the northside road and the cliffs, was across Indian Creek from their camp.

They lived in a colony of half-wood, half-canvas structures. As far as the officials were concerned, the structures were unsightly and unhealthy, and needed to be replaced. "Uncle Sam," symbolized by Superintendent Charles Goff Thomson, decided upon a totally new Indian Village in an out-of-sight area.

By 1933, thirteen three-room and six-room cabins, a central wash house, and a six-car garage had been built for the Indians west of Yosemite Lodge. "They moved reluctantly," John Reymann

stated. "They didn't want to leave the creek and their traditional outdoor way of life."

These surviving Native Americans also objected to paying rent, and being restricted to how many visitors they could have and how long the visitors could stay. When asked if he was bitter at being raised in a segregated village, Jay Johnson, now a forestry foreman for the Park Service, answered, "I wasn't then, but now I am."

Charlie Castro has happy memories. "The Indian Village was a special area where live music was always present, and the monthly potlucks were always fun. I remember my mother [Agnes Tom Castro] calling me in at night as I sat up listening to music and watching the young women sing familiar tunes. The big times were when relatives would visit from the east side. There was always plenty to eat. I remember my mother making dozens of enchiladas, tortillas, and lots of beans. There was plenty of deer meat, and acorn and mulligan stew. I helped by gathering the acorns and sometimes shelling them."

"I remember seeing the Indian children arrive at school, having walked the mile plus from the Indian Village," Stewart Cramer wrote. "I don't

Tabuce (Maggie Howard) was paid $2.00 a day and allowed to sell the baskets and beadwork she made to the public. (Mariposa Museum and History Center Collection)

coordinated by the time they were six or eight years old, than their white counterparts.

"I can honestly say that my relations with Indian children were no better or worse than with the white children."

Cramer still feels that the segregated housing increased the immense social and cultural gulf between the Indians and the white residents.

The two best-known residents of the Indian Village were Chris Brown and Maggie Howard, whom the admiring public knew as Lemee and Tabuce. After a replica Indian camp—complete with native dwellings, acorn granaries, a sweat house, and even a rock with grinding holes—was placed back of the museum, Maggie was hired by the Park Service to demonstrate how Indian women gathered and prepared food, selected materials, and made intricately-woven baskets for varying uses. Her skill and sweet face made her popular with adults and children.

Betty Haigh "watched Tabuce by the hour" during summer afternoons. "I was always amazed at her sense of time. She never wore a

remember them owning bicycles—often not too well dressed. They carried sack lunches, but occasionally nothing at all.

"The Indian children who attended the Yosemite school, descendants of Chief Tenaya, exemplified the basic, natural law of 'survival of the fittest.' They were stronger, faster, and better

Among others, Leah Ashworth, Betty Cookson, Sally Knowles, Betty Jobe, and Winifred Hilton danced around a Maypole about 1937. (Betty Jobe Sargent Collection)

watch, but every day at 2 o'clock she'd reach in her pocket and take a dime out of a wrinkled handkerchief and tell me to go buy us ice cream cones. I was the only child honored by such a commission, and I tell you I was proud!"

Another child who knew Maggie and the chief well was Bob McCabe, now an architect and artist. "I was eleven in 1938 when I first watched Chief Lemee perform his native dancing against replicas of the original Indian structures with Half Dome looming in the background to the east and Yosemite Falls almost directly behind. Tabuce was sitting quietly aside weaving on her now famous baskets. Our entire family was fascinated by the total performance."

During the next two summers, Bob explained, "I occupied our campsite by myself except for weekends, when my sisters and parents came up from Fresno laden with food and supplies. My parents had arranged with Chief Lemee to supervise my weekday activities so I reported to him each morning. If I didn't participate in any of the Park Ranger guided hikes to Half Dome, Glacier Point, the top of Yosemite Falls, etc., I would spend the day at the Indian Village behind the Park museum with Lemee and Tabuce.

"During these periods Chief Lemee found many activities to keep my interest, including teaching me how to chip obsidian into arrowheads, hunting for colorful orange and black flicker feathers for his dance masks and hawk and owl feathers for his cape, and assisting him with putting on his costume.

"When Tabuce was running low on her supply of material for weaving, she and the Chief would show me the materials to be gathered and teach me how to cut and bundle, prune and strip the different vegetation from the valley floor.

"I learned the dance steps from Lemee by observation, and the chants from hearing them repeated numerous times. I also learned a few individual words that they used to communicate between themselves.

"I was fascinated by both the making of the dance costumes and the facial and body painting. The painted designs seemed to change on an almost daily basis. I was more interested in how to chip obsidian using a deer horn and buckskin hand pad than I was in assembling the total

Chris Brown was a great favorite as Chief Lemee. (Mariposa Museum and History Center Collection)

arrow, including the Chief's primitive way of fletching.

"I was also fascinated with the process of basket construction and particularly how the designs varied and seemed to come directly from Tabuce's mind to the weaving instead of some method of graphically predesigning the intricate patterns. To keep me busy, Tabuce started me on pine needle baskets. My skills seemed to be in cutting obsidian, and I lacked the ability and patience needed for basket weaving."

Today a small obsidian arrowhead that Lemee "carved from a piece of rare red obsidian" for Bob is among his most prized possessions. So are his "fond memories of the six years of opportunity to spend my summers mainly with my Indian family

Nancy Loncaric with her "bumblebees in a flower garden" in May 1939. Left to right: Raye LaVonn Shorb, Eleanor Carr, —— Carr, Nola June Jacobs, Joan Wosky, Suzanne McKown, and Charlotte Ewing. (Charlotte Ewing Collection)

in my favorite place in the world, Yosemite."

From 1917 until 1956, when a modern school was built, the little red schoolhouse for Yosemite's children wasn't red at all, but a high-roofed yellow and brown shingled affair with two classrooms, one with a stage concealed behind heavy drapes. The "big room" held the big kids, fifth through eighth grades, and the "little room" housed the first through fourth graders. By 1938, John "Duke" Merriman said, "There were more little kids than big so the big and little kids traded rooms."

"Coats and overshoes and lunches were kept in the 'cloakroom' that always smelled of wet wool and banana peels," Mary Jane Degen wrote, "and your name was over your coat hook."

In the late 1930s, Jane McKown reflected, "We had to write our name on the blackboard when we needed to visit the restroom. Seems archaic now. There was a white line painted down the hall and because I was pigeon-toed, I was excused for a short time each morning and afternoon to walk down that line, trying to keep a foot on each side—pointed straight ahead. I doubt if it cured anything but it was a nice break for me."

Teachers, most of them good, came and went. Everett Harwell has an indelible memory of the upper-grades teacher in 1930. "I don't recall his name, but he had a habit of saying loud enough for the whole room to hear, 'That's tee-totally wrong!' much to the chagrin of the errant pupil."

At that time, a Miss Bell presided over the "little room." Later, Lenore Knoblock had the older grades, and Maud Hicks the wigglers.

After John Loncaric began work for the Curry Company in 1930, the school gained a volunteer music teacher. At first his energetic, vivacious, and talented wife, Nancy, gave piano lessons, but, she remembered in 1992 at age ninety-two, "As the school had no music, the Mariposa County School Superintendent asked if I would give them some time. I said, 'Yes, if you let me do it my way, and not just sing songs. I want to teach them about good music, opera, etc.' He laughed, and gave permission."

Assisted by a ranger's wife, Millie Anderson, Nancy would go to the school "two or three times a week and play the piano while we sang songs," Mary Degen elaborated. "Those two women directed many a play or program, usually starting with the little ones singing and then playing in Mrs. Loncaric's 'Rhythm Band.' We'd wear costumes made out of cardboard and crepe paper, and then the big kids would recite poems and

Built in 1917, this school served Yosemite until it was replaced in 1956.
(YRL Collection)

for all sorts of events, even at the Ahwahnee. Each child had a simple instrument—bells, drums, things to shake. I was always proud of anything the children did, little or big. Music was my life."

Beverly Wagner and her brother Jim were both members of the noise-making band. "Everyone wanted to play the triangles," Bev remembered, "and no one liked sandblocks or rhythm sticks."

Charlie Castro loved to beat the drums. "I began to play drums on my mother's pots and pans when I was old enough to hold sticks. Music was always part of my life."

"I remember Mrs. Loncaric playing the Warsaw Concerto to the Camp Curry audience one summer,"Bette Waddington recorded. "It was really thrilling.
She also took the trouble to play the piano part to some of my violin pieces and did everything so graciously, so kindly and with such wisdom that she made an impression that has guided my life. My other inspiration was Yosemite and I

sing more songs. Sometimes there would be a play, and the programs always started off with the salute to the flag, that only had forty-eight stars, and the salute that did not have the words 'under God' in it."

"The Rhythm Band was a big event in Yosemite," Nancy Loncaric continued. "They played

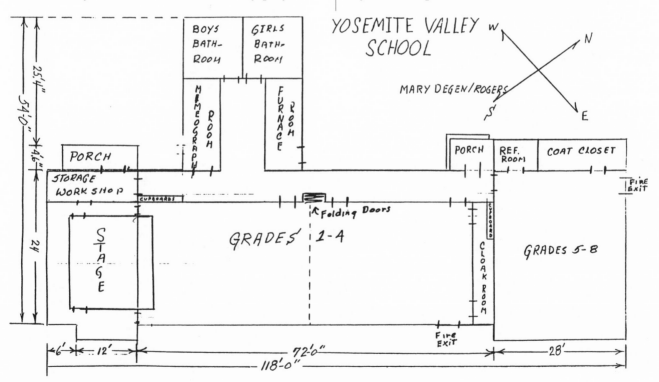

Floor plan of the Yosemite Elementary School, pictured above. (By Mary Degen Rogers)

managed to practice in view of Yosemite Falls."

In 1958, Bette, a graduate of the Juilliard School of Music, became a violinist with the St. Louis Symphony Orchestra, for which she still plays.

"Recess was the best time of the day," according to Mary. "Games ran the gamut from Keep-away, tag, baseball, Annie-Annie-Over, Red Rover, jump rope, kick-the-can, jacks, and tic-tac-toe. The 'teacherage' and the garage next to it were a great place to play 'Annie-Annie-Over' except when Jack Leidig, who said he was the oldest man in Yosemite (we thought he was the oldest man in the world), was a temporary janitor. He'd yell 'Don't throw the ball on the roof!' which, of course, made us do it all the more."

School custodian Ernie Collins was a favorite with the students. Any child staying after school for some reason would be entertained watching Ernie draw "pictures on the board with a wet rag as he cleaned the blackboards," was one of Mary's memories. "You also got to clap the erasers outside if you wanted to help him."

Ballerinas Jane McKown, Eleanor Carr, Doris ——, Joan Van Hosen, Janet Alaird, Carol ——, Donna Alexander, and Jane Wosky, dressed or undressed, for a May 1937 performance. (Jane McKown Chapman Collection)

Rich Hodges liked Ernie for two reasons. "I remember barely staggering to school, only half awake and really cold. There wasn't much room in Ernie's furnace room, but it was warm and the blast of the oil-fired furnace hypnotized me till school started.

"If one had a great taste for a 7-Up, candy bar

Neither Ranger Bill Reymann nor the captive deer approved of the Yosemite Zoo. (YRL Collection)

Fred Alexander's daughter June with her pet fawn. (YP & CC Collection)

"I learned to play drums by listening to records of bands like Benny Goodman, the Dorsey brothers, etc. This also gave me a chance to play with the local guys at the Indian Village, with the Rhythm Band, and in a little jazz band organized by a woman named Gladys Adams. My dad bought me a set of used drums when I was ten." Today Charlie is a forester and expert on tree hazard management for the Park Service, as well as a professional drummer for the High Sierra Jazz Band. The band has played in many different states and in various foreign countries.

Some residents felt that Yosemite was provincial, but parents as well as teachers united in seeing that the children received not only a good education, but varied experiences. One field trip to the El Portal railroad station was never forgotten by Dick Otter, then in the first grade.

"We toured the engine and each of us got to pull the cord that blew the whistle. At the end of the trip we were each given engineers' caps and a pin that said we were Junior Engineers."

Thanks to the ranger naturalists, there was no lack of experts on wildlife, trees, glaciology, astronomy, and birds to interest the local children in natural history and science. Chief naturalist Bert Harwell was especially popular because he would teach them how to whistle bird calls when he took them on nature walks.

At least once, according to Dick Otter, students had an intimate classroom demonstration in the ways of nature. "One of my fellow students returned after a lengthy illness. In her absence a mouse had made a nest in her desk and given birth to several young.[1] The teacher called all of the students from the other classroom, and we watched while the mother carried each of her babies out of the desk and into the heating grate."

Mary Degen recalled the time "when we were

or gum as I did, and the usual places, under the back porch of the old Lodge and along the horse trail by Yosemite Falls, yielded nothing, you went to Ernie. He paid a nickel apiece for cleaning blackboards, a dime apiece for cleaning the girls or boys bathrooms, and a magnificent quarter apiece for sweeping the big or little rooms. I got nothing unless I did a good job.

"Ernie was responsible for keeping the Post Office clean too, and sweeping its floor was worth a quarter. I really preferred the Post Office because careless tourists dropped coins on the floor."

Later, Ernie taught Charlie Castro how to clean the school properly. "Soon he paid me to help him with his work. As I became more responsible, he paid me to clean the main Post Office at night." Charlie put a lot of miles on his bike riding between the Indian Village and the school or Post Office, and to Camp Curry in the summers. "Big bands from San Francisco and Los Angeles were booked for the nightly dances. Jack Petty and his orchestra from S.F. was the best.

1. Phyllis Reinhart recalled, "Opening my desk after a holiday, I found a nest of hairless mice, whose parents had gone down my inkwell to build their home."

studying about airplanes (or maybe it was careers), the teacher sent away for Junior Pilot and Junior Stewardess pins . . . and we were all going to grow up to be pilots or stewardesses."

Chief Lemee and Tabuce came to school to demonstrate tribal dances and costumes.

Ballroom dancing and everything from the fox trot to jitterbug, Charlie remembered, were taught by the Womacks, who worked for the Curry Company late in the Depression but were professional dancers. Dancing lessons were also given by Stewart Cramer's mother, and by Annette Zaepffel. Mornings she taught the three R's to the lower grades; afternoons she taught ballroom dancing and a variety of folk dances to the upper grades.

Yosemite Elementary had never boasted a kindergarten, and when the Mariposa County Supervisors were approached during the Depression, no funds were available. "So," artist Della Taylor Hoss explained, "several of us mothers of kindergarten eligibles set out to create one. Virginia Best Adams was my greatest helper."

The Curry Company donated the space—initially a roofed porch at the old Yosemite Lodge. Virginia Oliver, daughter of the resident U.S. Courts Commissioner, "had just finished her kindergarten training and was willing to teach the first year, *nobly* for the modest sum of $2.00 per child."

Funds were raised at a successful bingo party at The Ahwahnee, "and we were able to launch the kindergarten in the Fall, 1937, with plenty of materials, elemental musical instruments and about twelve eager children. Among them were Pete Hoss, Mike Adams, Dick Otter, Paul dePfyffer, and the Hooley twins, Nancy and Bart."

Unhappily for the founder's son, Pete Hoss, he had to "endure" a second year of the pre-school, "Because," he said, "I was born ten days too late to enter first grade with my kindergarten classmates and inseparable buddies, Mike Adams and Dick Otter. I do not know who made the rule or why, but it undoubtedly contributed to a life-long distaste for bureaucracy."

Justice triumphed when, after three weeks in the first grade, he "was skipped to the second and reunited with Mike" by teacher Gayle Tarnutzer.

Perhaps that incident contributed to Pete's later study and practice of law.

Another "lack," a sports program, was perceived and remedied in 1939, when "My father (accountant Sterling S. Cramer) organized the Yosemite Football Team," son Stewart recorded. "We practiced in a clearing, where there were only a few trees and boulders, near the foot of the Four-Mile Trail." That area had been the site of Leidig's Hotel and, later, Camp Ahwahnee.

"A similar team (age limit fourteen or under) had been organized in Mariposa where we played our first game, on the old sawdust-covered field at the high school. We lost 48 to nothing."

Later a regulation playing field was created adjacent to the Yosemite School. The team became the Yosemite Badgers, and occasionally scored a touchdown, but, Mike Adams commented, "Whether we played an eleven-man or a six-man team, we always lost to Mariposa!"

The Badgers were hard-pressed to field an eleven-boy team, and they lacked reserves because, although the student body had increased to around eighty, only a few were old enough or strong enough to play. Yosemite Elementary, however, excelled at winter sports as a team and individually. Leroy "Rusty" Rust and his tremendous accomplishments while at the elementary school and at Mariposa High was a source of pride to the student body. He won a silver medal in a race on only his second time on snowshoes. When he took up tennis, he waited until after Camp Curry closed in the fall, then practiced his serve by hitting balls against the concrete walls of the empty swimming pool.

Once the Badger Pass Ski Area opened, in 1935, Rusty began collecting trophies for wins in downhill and slalom races. During the 1934–35 school year, his last year at Yosemite Elementary, he was the social studies chairman as well as editor of the school's newspaper. While at Mariposa High he won a baseball scholarship to Stanford, but couldn't use it because he wrenched his knee playing football. On and off the athletic fields, Rusty's even-tempered good nature, his ability to laugh at himself, and his contagious joy in life and his love of Yosemite, made him a legion of friends. As an adult, he was also known for his outspoken defense of anything or anybody

Bill Lintott, Jeanne Brandon, Marilyn Moen, Bette Jobe, Winifred Hilton, Sally Knowles, Velda Johnson, John Telles, and Ken Carpenter (not shown), composed the large eighth grade graduating class in 1937. Teacher Lenore Knoblock is in the middle. (Betty Jobe Sargent Collection)

that threatened Yosemite.[2]

Rusty's love of winter sports was shared by Stewart Cramer, who couldn't resist the thrill of tobogganing. "Between the Camp Curry cabins and LeConte Memorial Lodge stood the Toboggan Slide—a timber ramp some hundred yards long. Each winter for more than two decades, by day or by night under floodlights, the Toboggan Slide provided locals with a stomach-churning descent over the boulders."

Before launching herself from the top of the slide, "Zip, about 60 miles an hour" in 1935, Barbara Van Housen, then twelve, took time to appreciate the view. "Right ahead of us is Half Dome. On one side of Half Dome is Clouds Rest. Every afternoon at four o'clock, clouds come and rest."

At age eleven, Sally Knowles thought that riding on a sled tied to the back of a horse-drawn sleigh was the best fun. Both girls wrote about winter for a school assignment; later their reactions were printed in the school's mimeographed "Yosemite Journal."

Plain old sledding held hazards, Marvin North testified. "One of my playmates was John Degen, and one day we decided to ride a sled off the snow on a big rock. John was in front and I on the back. Anyway, we crashed near the bottom, I got a broken leg and I think John lost a tooth or two."

When Betty Hoffman was in the eighth grade she wrote about skating for the school newspaper.

---

2. Rusty's seventy-one year longevity in Yosemite was interrupted only by attendance at Fresno State, and a year in the army. (An attack of scarlet fever led to a medical discharge.) His love of skiing and children, including his own daughter and son, made him an outstanding coach-chauffeur-cook and all-around everything to generations of what he fondly called "crappy kids,"—better known as the Yosemite Ski Team. His twenty-eight year career as the Park's postmaster earned him the title of "Mr. 95389," and he referred to himself as a middle-class millionaire because of the environment, job, and friends. More than 500 of his friends attended an outdoor wake at Badger Pass several months after his cancer-caused death in January 1992. Showers fell during part of the program, prompting one admirer to say that they were caused by Rusty's tears because he couldn't be "with us."

"Ice skating usually opens around the first of December and closes about the 26th of February. People come from all over to skate that have never ever tried before."

"That wonderful, vast, outdoor rink," Lloyd Kramer claims, "was a far different experience than the recent rinky dink set up. I watched Leroy Rust win his skating championships on the old rink, his pairs championships with Catherine Lally, and I watched lots of collegiate hockey." Teams from schools as distant as the University of Southern California competed in Yosemite.

"Rusty" Rust, on the left, and two companions, burning up the ice. (YRL Collection)

Downhill skiing at the Badger Pass Ski Area was more easily mastered by the children than by the Yosemite adults. Not every young-ster succumbed to the exhilaration of flying down the slopes. Pete Hoss "was not into skiing as a child.I was afraid of it." As an adult, however, "I got the bug, and I have not quit since."

Skis were primitive, as was the non-high-fashion dress. "We wore wide-bottomed Norwegian ski-pants bloused at the ankle," Stewart Cramer recalled, "with wool socksturned down over the tops of our square-toed, semi-flexible, leather ski boots."

Until 1948 there wasn't a single modern ski-lift at Badger. "We rode to the top of the Big Hill in the Up-ski, a barge-like sled pulled by a cable," Stewart continued. "We loaded our skis and poles into the rack and held on tightly, standing as we rode. We knew we were halfway up when we passed the second sled, on its way down in the adjacent track." These pioneer conveyances were called Big Bertha and Queen Mary, and were considered by youthful riders such as Darrol Born to be "very modern devices."

10

The Great Flood

IN DECEMBER of 1937, snow was scant even at Badger Pass, but an onslaught of warm, torrential rain on Thursday the eighth soon melted what little there was. Over eleven inches of rain pelted down before the storm ceased, causing a flood of unprecedented extent. Much of Yosemite Valley became a lake several feet deep.

Because of the downpour and the advent of Christmas vacation, Mariposa High let out early on Friday, but not early enough. By the time the school bus, a Curry Company bus, and an aging pickup reached Cascade Creek, the bridge had washed out. Eighteen-year-old Al Gordon was driving himself and sister Gladys home to Wawona in the truck, and vividly remembers the consternation, deluge, and noise. "We watched the CCC boys, whose camp near the Merced's edge was in grave danger, fell a couple of good-sized pine trees across the creek, which had become a river. The camp manager had the boys lash the trees together with cable and covered with 2 x 12 planks."

It was risky, but all three vehicles inched across and slowly followed a bulldozer that was pushing rocks off the road. In some places water was running over the rock wall bordering the road. The Gordons reached Wawona after dark, and found that the bridge spanning the South Fork was damaged but passable.

That night several high schoolers celebrated at the superintendent's home, hosted by his son, Lawrence Merriman, Jr. Lawrence Merriman, Sr. had taken over after Superintendent Charles Goff Thomson's death in April 1937.

"It rained so hard," Larry recalled, "there was concern about getting everyone home. Our yard backed up to Yosemite Creek and wasn't far from the Merced River and both were roaring and almost over their banks.

"The next morning I looked out my bedroom window to see the back porch float away! The creek and the river seemed to meet at our house. Dad told us to pack some clothes as we must leave at once. John Wosky, Assistant Superintendent, came over to help us get out to the high ground. We went to the Ranger's Club in Government Center, a great lark for two boys in company with the single rangers and "Fitz" Fitzpatrick, the Assistant Postmaster. I was much impressed with all the happenings, how much water was in the valley, what was flooded and the size of the waterfalls. The Gallison lawn was ruined by a rock slide at their house near the cliffs.

"In the meantime the water was getting higher; my father and a couple of other men took a boat to our place to move furniture and loose items upstairs. He had a very busy time coordinating all the damage reports and relief efforts. At least one man, Mr. McCain, was badly hurt by a falling pine tree in Ahwahnee Meadow."[1]

Ranger's son Bob Skakel, who slept in the attic because his prized electric train was laid out there, looked out the window about 7:00 A.M. on the eleventh "and couldn't believe what I saw. Water was almost up to the main road that went from the Lodge to Government Center.

"I went and called Dad who didn't quite believe me until he got up, looked out and said, 'My God!' That was the beginning of what I thought was a great time even though our house was out

---

1. B. H. (Bike) McCain, a Bureau of Public Roads engineer, received facial cuts when the tree fell on his truck, crushing the hood and breaking the windshield. His daughters, Pat and Joanne, attended Yosemite Elementary.

Although the flood of 1937 was exceeded by those of 1950 and 1955, it created an impressive lake. (Stewart Cramer Collection)

came down and got us in some trucks and took us up to the Lodge. We all stayed there together and it was fun."

Fellow refugee Jay Johnson agreed. "It was exciting. Yosemite Falls was huge. You could feel spray clear down at the Lodge."

Teenaged Della Dondero was less thrilled. For some reason, she and her grandmother, Louisa Tom, who was over ninety, had to walk—almost wade—to the Lodge.

"To me, only three," Charlie Castro said, "it seemed as if the entire rock wall above us was one gigantic waterfall. It was very dark, water running everywhere, rocks falling. Large slides made the ground shake."

Mary Degen and Beverley June Riddle also remembered the frightening noise of landslides, and rocks crashing down near their houses.

Suzanne and Jane McKown, young daughters of the Park Service's landscape architect, witnessed the flood's rearrangement of the landscape as "mountains of water and debris poured down the cliffs in back of our place (below Sunnyside Ledge) and streams ran down the driveway. My father and another ranger grabbed my sister and me from our beds and took us down to Yosemite Lodge," is Suzanne's memory. "We slept on the floor with many people—quite exciting!"

of power, and without any heat. I remember watching tent frames floating down the river.

"What was really comical was watching some of the resident ranger-naturalists going around with gunny sacks, picking up the moles and gophers that were being driven out of their holes by rising water. That was far from a life saving mission; the rodents were needed to feed all the snakes on exhibit at the Museum."

Although the main buildings at Yosemite Lodge were safe, its numerous, widely-scattered cabins were flooded. A couple of the lowest cabins at the Indian Village "had water in 'em," according to Ralph Parker, then seven. "They

Altogether, damage to the Park's roads, trails, bridges (seventeen trail bridges in the Valley alone were washed away), campgrounds, and buildings—particularly the superintendent's house—amounted to $272,000. The Curry Company's loss was about $150,000, a lot of that because of the general store and employee housing in Old Village.

"We didn't have to evacuate," said Stewart Cramer, then seven, "because our house, the old Chinese laundry, and the Patterson's next to us, formerly the ice house, stood on rocky, rising ground a few hundred feet from rickety old Cedar Cottage.

"I woke up several times during the night of the eleventh when my father came home to change into dry clothing. He and some other men had stretched a rope from the front of the Old Village Store, across the road to the front of Degnan's Store and Restaurant, and to this rope they fastened our battered old rowboat. All night they ran the boat back and forth across the road, carrying items for an emergency food supply.

"My father had salvaged this rowboat from the Curry dump, and had propped it up in our back yard for my friends and me to play in. It was completely unseaworthy to begin with, and its use on the night of the high water finished it off, once and for all!

"After my father and the other men had cached a supply of food which they had brought across the road from the Old Village Store in our old rowboat, and departed the area, Jack Patterson and Oscar returned and brought the boat across the road one more time to the front of the store, and filled it up with liquor bottles.

"Next, using some kind of poles, for there weren't any oars, they poled the boat upstream, through the water that covered the road—which would have been primarily the backwash along the south shore at this time—in an attempt to reach the Curry Company stables where Oscar was living.

"They were somewhere in the middle of Camp 16 when the boat hit a snag, and they had to abandon ship. This is what finally happened to our old, battered rowboat. My father said that they spent the night in a tree, and were rescued the next morning by people in a motorboat.

"My memory of Yosemite Valley, the next day, consists mainly of a scene resembling the Mississippi River, with logs, picnic tables, and other objects floating downriver at high speed. Only the four stone towers of the Sentinel Bridge extended

Moving Day for one of the many WOBs—rooms without bath—at Yosemite Lodge in 1937. (Stewart Cramer Collection)

above the water. The river stopped short of our front steps."[2]

The worst storm casualty was the CCC camp between the river and Cascade Fall. Four of the large barracks and the officers quarters were swept away, and both the mess hall and the recreation building were damaged beyond repair. When full, the camp housed more than 100 men; most of them escaped to El Portal on foot, forming human chains while wading through flooded stretches of the road.

Teenager Audrey Beck saw them arrive, soaked, still scared, and exhausted. They were fed and housed in the hotel and the El Portal School. By the twentieth, most of the men were at work on clean-up, repair work, and cutting firewood to replace the piles that had been swept downriver from their former camp. A new campsite was selected between the northside road and the talus slopes immediately west of the checking station at the bottom of the Control Road. Construction

2. Some of the text by Stewart Cramer first appeared in *Sierra Escape,* published twice a year by Susan M. Shaughnessy in Midpines, California. Permission to reprint parts of Cramer's articles was given by him and by the publisher.

Another casualty was the Village store. (Stewart Cramer Collection)

"There were all sorts of canned food," Bob said, "but the labels had washed off. So no one knew what the heck was inside even though numbers were stamped on the tops.

"At nights, Mom would say, 'Well, what shall we have for dinner? How about can number X23Y?' We would make guesses as to contents. I remember guessing a big one to be peaches. Much to my dismay, it turned out to be canned peas which I hated."

Bob collected the Log Cabin syrup cans, not because of their sweet contents but because they made great additions to his electric train layout!

Toilet paper was in demand because it, and other paper goods, were strewn down the river, draped over shrubs, rocks, and small trees, unwound and unsalvageable. "Eventually," Bob added, "power was restored, and then eventually we were connected to the outside world." There was concern that many fish had been swept downriver by the flood, but on opening day of the 1938 season Bobby Gallison, age eleven, caught "fifteen and all of them were fat."

Before that, Christmas came. Thanks largely to Mary and Don Tresidder, who regretted being childless, and other young-at-heart parents, a special party in the Pavilion and later in the dining room at Camp Curry, was planned for months ahead of time. The flood of 1937 complicated the celebration but did not stop it.

Preparations had begun in the fall when the first graders through fourth graders wrote "want" letters to Santa. Mrs. Santa, Mary Tresidder, read them carefully, then tried "her best to find the requests from little red wagons to an atlas! She took great pains to see that every child received fine presents," recalled Della Hoss, who helped Mrs. T., as she was known locally, shop for the gifts in Fresno and the Bay Area.

"We were treated right," Ralph Parker said. "Once I got skis."

"I must have written a hell of a pathetic letter

was begun early in 1938. Meanwhile, the dispossessed men and those at the Wawona CCC camp did yeoman rehabilitation work at both places.

Even though the rain finally ceased on the twelfth, and "Lake Yosemite" receded, the Valley itself was still isolated. Both the All-Year Highway and the Wawona Road had washed out, so traffic could not move in or out. Train service was halted for eighteen months while more than 30,000 feet of railroad track were replaced. Sterling Cramer's salvaged food helped, but there were definite shortages in the Valley. Enterprising lads such as Bob Skakel splashed over to the meadow west of the Old Village Store and warehouse, where residents picked through the soggy merchandise.

in 1937," Bob Skakel said, "saying that I knew it was my last chance since I was in fourth grade, and I really, REALLY wanted electric switches for my Lionel train! I put down tennis racket for second choice, something I hadn't the least desire or need for.

"Well, of course the flood caused problems for acquisition and delivery because the railroad didn't run for months. Anyway, at the annual party, my name was called and what do I get? A Spaulding tennis racket and a box of balls. I'm sure Santa could see my chin dragging on the ground 'cuz he knew all of us kids."

Snow began to fall on Christmas Eve, and Bob was up early the next morning. "I ran outside to the covered porch to see all the beautiful snow and there on the bench was a package for me. I raced inside to open it and, my gosh, there was the set of switches from Santa!"

"That was the highlight of my Christmas,

and later my folks found out that it was Mary Tresidder who had delivered that package, snow or no snow."

In Mary Degen's opinion, Santa with pure white hair and beard, thick red velvet suit trimmed with white fur, black leather belt with a gold buckle, and knee-high black leather boots, "was pure magic to a kid." Later "I was told that Dr. Don Tresidder was Santa, but I'll never believe that! I remember getting a wooden doll house full of furniture one year, and a Shirley Temple doll another time. Santa never failed."

Tresidder was also popular with children for his exuberant, generous, non-Santa self. He had a beautiful palomino horse, and often took local children with him for rides that were much coveted—but not by little Peter Hoss. "I never wanted to go. Once I finally did and came back, and told my parents, "Well, now that's over!"

Pete was among the proud band of Yosemite

When this picture was taken, in 1934, the CCC boys at the Cascade Camp were enjoying the river, but in December 1937 the flood-swollen Merced swept away all the large buildings in the background, leaving the boys homeless and frightened. (YRL Collection)

babies, those fortunate to have been born in Lewis Memorial Hospital and delivered by Dr. Hartley Dewey during his 1929–1942 tenure as medical director, or by his greatly loved successor, Dr. Avery Sturm, who was there from 1934 to 1971. Pete's birth in April 1934 was the first at which Dr. Sturm assisted with a Yosemite baby. There were many more. Nancy and Barton Hooley were born twenty minutes apart at Lewis Memorial in July of 1935. Nancy believes that "ours was the first multiple birth in the Valley." Partly because their father was a ski instructor, the twins learned to ski at the age of three.

"If you were born in Yosemite," Pete has insisted for years, "you never completely adjust to the outside world. Parents tell city kids to be home before dark; I was told to come when the last of the alpen glow left the rocky summit of Half Dome.

"While deer and bear were common sights in Yosemite, I would marvel at cows or neon lights when we would go out of the Valley."

In some ways, Yosemite was insulated from the Great Depression, but travel and revenue decreased sharply. In 1934, the worst year, the Curry Company's net profit was a bit under $1,500! Nevertheless, Santa Claus arrived laden with gifts, and Mom, Dad, or a grandparent received a paycheck. No one could live in Yosemite without at least one member of each household being employed in the Valley. "Many resident children welcomed the lack of tourists," Mary Degen said, "whom they resented for intruding on *their* Valley. We didn't understand that visitors were our livelihood. We loved to tell each other about dumb things some 'dude' had said or done.

"I don't remember being poor. But later Mom said that Dad (a carpenter for the Curry Company) was making three dollars a day. We 'made do,' and no one told us we were poor."

"My father was Yosemite's shoe repairman from 1932 to 1942," Lloyd Kramer wrote, "and he did some fine oil portraits on the side. We lived about half the time in a tent cabin with no plumbing. I didn't know at that time that we were very poor, so I had a wonderful time."

Results of medical tests taken of fifty-four pupils late in 1935 suggest, however, that a Depression diet may have affected their health.

Building benches from logs was just one of the many beneficial projects tackled by the CCC. (YRL Collection)

A bicycle brigade of local children followed President Franklin D. Roosevelt's limousine as he was driven around Yosemite Valley on July 15, 1938. (YRL Collection)

Thirty-five of them were underweight, twenty-one had infected tonsils, and nineteen had bad teeth.

It seems safe to assume that the PTA and the public relations departments of both the park administration and the concessionaire worked closely together to provide special occasions for Yosemite's isolated youngsters. "Jack Benny's greeting to us kids was his radio trademark, 'Jello again,'" Charlotte Ewing reminisced. "He was a character, and made us all laugh."

Mary Degen laughed until Benny "told my best friend, Beverly, that she looked like his daughter. Boy, was I jealous!"[3]

When President Franklin D. Roosevelt was driven through the Valley in 1938, his Cadillac convertible was escorted by a phalanx of local bike-riding children. "I wonder what the Secret Servicemen thought of us," Charlotte marveled. "No one stopped us and the president waved."

By then the Kramer family, Lloyd said, "had graduated to a small 'real' house just across from

3. Both girls were born in the Yosemite hospital on the same day, which, they later felt, destined them to be best friends. They were, and still are!

the village store, where my dad worked. From there I watched Franklin Roosevelt being driven by in his open car. He didn't realize that the real crowd was on the store side of the road, so he waved warmly at me and our family." Lloyd, whose career was to be that of a director of university libraries, began his Horatio Alger saga in Yosemite. "Before I was of employable age I caught grasshoppers and sold them to fishermen (twenty-five cents a can full). Later I distributed the *Yosemite News,* a company newsletter, by bicycle, for the princely sum of one dollar for each issue.

"For a short time I worked as a courier for film, doing a bicycle run from the Old Village store to Camp Curry where film was developed. And at the annual Fourth of July rodeo, held near the Sentinel Hotel, where Don Tresidder paraded ceremoniously on his palomino, I sold soda pop. One of the not inconsiderable fringe benefits of

this employment was leave to drink as much of the stuff as I could consume. It was in connection with this job that I obtained my Social Security card, which I still carry, with the Camp 6 address on it. Later I worked as a porter at Camp Curry, did some work as a porter at the Lodge, worked as a dishwasher and later busboy at the Ahwahnee, busboy at Badger Pass, and dishwasher at the old hotel at Glacier Point. The work as a porter was enormously remunerative and served, along with the GI Bill, to put me through college."

The job market for teenage girls was more restrictive, Mary Degen testified. "On my sixteenth birthday, Patti Brown and I got jobs bussing dishes at the old Lodge cafeteria. Minimum wage was 55¢ an hour, but we were told that since we lived with our parents in the Valley, we'd be paid 50¢ an hour. We accepted. Equal pay and gender discrimination were unknown terms then."

Even in Yosemite, Shirley Temple films and

Children and adults alike paraded over to the Ranger's Club to have their pictures taken with the famous movie star. Shirley Temple Black has revisited Yosemite numerous times, at least once to participate in the annual Christmas-time bird count. (Suzanne McKown Turnquist Collection)

look-alike dolls were well-known in the 1930s. Consequently her appearance at a reception given in her honor at the Rangers Club attracted a crowd of children and adults. Many pictures were taken of the radiantly-smiling movie star with different groups. Fourth grader Richie Hodges said that when the excited youngsters were a bit disorderly, Shirley admonished, "Now children, let's all be ladies and gentlemen."

That was a constant refrain from parents in trying to temper their offspring's wild and free image. The Ahwahnee Hotel, the epitome of a castle, was a training ground for manners. Perhaps in lieu of baby-sitters, there was a children's table set aside for any child lucky enough to accompany parents for a meal in the vast dining room. "Awe kept us subdued as much as all the parental admonitions to be little ladies and gentlemen," was Charlotte's memory.

Soon after "my parents (Helen and Sterling

Litter-bearers Dick Russell and Stewart Cramer carrying in the boar's head for one of the famous Bracebridge Dinners. (Stewart Cramer Collection)

Cramer) and I moved to the Valley in 1935," Stewart recorded, "Mother was invited to afternoon tea at The Ahwahnee. I was only four and a half, but she told me later that as she was introduced to Colonel Thomson, the park superintendent, everyone's attention was diverted to where I was standing on my head."

Ten or so years later, a more gentlemanly Stewart was back at the Ahwahnee to take part in the annual Christmas Bracebridge Dinner pageant. Based upon one of Washington Irving's tales, it was expanded and elaborated upon with splendid music by the versatile Ansel Adams, who also directed, photographed, and starred in it as Lord of Misrule. The Tresidders portrayed the Squire and his Lady, Virginia Best Adams was the housekeeper, and Herman Hoss the sonorous Parson. The Bracebridge, begun in 1927, is still a famous Yosemite tradition.

Yosemite's teenagers filled minor roles. "As a Servitor, for a few years I helped bring in the Flaming Plum Pudding and 'Sir Loin, Baron of Beef,' and once, the Boar's Head," Stewart recalled.

Winter festivities and sports were enjoyed by Yosemite's younger generation, but spring and summer vacation symbolized freedom and the opportunity to camp, climb, and explore all over the Park. Suzanne McKown treasures the memory of a moonlight trek with her father to the top of Half Dome when she was twelve. "It was a thrilling experience to climb up holding on the cables on the dome itself—one I can hardly stand to think of now."

Ev Harwell's first fishing and backpack trip in 1931 was with his inseparable friend Herb Ewing. "We were at Merced Lake by ourselves for two weeks when we were twelve."

Darrol Born's outstanding memories are related to the seasons. "They include swimming in the Merced, skating at Camp Curry, flying down the toboggan slide and ash can alley, and, of course, skiing at Badger Pass was the winter highlight. Also, I always thought the early days of September when school had started and the tourists gone, were truly great."

Little pleasures were important, too, naturalist's daughter Phyllis Cole confided. "Because we lived directly across the street from school, my sister and I awaited the bell's ringing before dashing out of the house. That was a plus! On the downside, I envied my friends who ate their sack lunches at school. It was a rare treat when Mother packed me a lunch to eat in the school yard."

Swimming in the river, bike riding everywhere, and wiener roasts were popular summer activities, now seen through rose-colored memories. Only one of the fifty-plus former children the author heard from described the annual spring torment of mosquitoes, their bites, and the aftereffects of itching, scratching, bleeding, and occasionally infection. Even today the pests are still here, but most of the breeding pools have been drained and "Off" is smeared on.

In contrast, most of the far-flung alumni had a bear story or two to tell. Bob Skakel and Mary Degen had the disconcerting experience of finding a bear peering in a window when they were peering out. While Pat Oliver was still in a crib in the front room of a tent cabin, a bear broke in the back door, waltzed into the kitchen, or middle room, for a tasty meat loaf. Unfortunately Pat's mother was in the back room, with the bear separating her from her infant. Mrs. Oliver's adrenal gland, and a handy broom, gave her the courage to rout the four-footed intruder.

And then there was a bear, or rather a boy-chased bear, that started a grass fire. Bruin was happily ensconced in an apple tree, chomping away on the fruit, when John Reymann and a friend tried vainly to get him out. "Don't ask me why we did that," John reminisced. "For fun, maybe. Finally we put some kerosene on a gunny sack, set it afire and gave that old bear a hot seat. WHOA, he got out of that tree all right, and ran to Yosemite Creek and dove in to cool off. The heck of it was, he had started a fire in the dry grass. Talk about trouble! Dad, Chief Ranger Townsley, the naturalists, they all piled on me. I was confined to the house and that was IT!"

Pat Phillips was surprised after she moved to the Park from a ranch because the Yosemite kids who had always lived in Yosemite would nonchalantly shoo off a bear, but were scared of dogs and sometimes ran if they saw one on a leash. Neither cats nor dogs were allowed in Yosemite, and visitors were supposed to place their pets in the Park kennels during their visits.

Pat and her brother Ted quickly learned to respect bears, and never to get "between cubs and a mother. So far as I know it was only the tourists who ever got hurt."

It was still Yosemite's age of innocence. In 1992, Ken Carpenter confessed, "To this day, I never lock the car and only with some effort do I remember to lock my house in Reno. Many, many years ago the company hired a new man. When he was shown the house he and his family were to live in he asked for a key. My father, as I remember it, had to bring in a locksmith from Merced to supply one. Great consternation!"

When he became sixteen, Ev Harwell was anxious to get his driver's license, but not sure as to the procedure. "One day Ranger Carl Danner climbed into my dad's Model A convertible and asked me to drive him to the store so he could buy a paper. That was my test."

Another sign of small-town atmosphere was the efficient telephone service. From a back-country phone, Ev explained, "You could crank a long or two shorts and the Valley operator would come on. After exchanging pleasantries with her, you'd say 'put me through to my dad at the museum or get me Herb.' If there was an after hours emergency, she could almost always tell you where the doctor was."

As late as 1952, as the author can testify, there was a surprising personal service inherent in the low-tech Yosemite system. My sister, Rosalie, in southern California, needed to notify my parents and me of an uncle's death, and we were staying near Big Meadow with no telephone. Rosalie told the Yosemite operator where we were, and finally said, desperately, "We have a ranger friend and I'm sure he'd take a message to them, but I can't remember his name."

"Can you describe him?" asked the obliging operator.

"No," admitted Rosalie, "but his daughter and I were in fourth grade together and her name was Nola June."

"Oh, you mean Jake!" the operator exclaimed, and within an hour Duane Jacobs had sent his wife up with the bad news.

11

Tuolumne Tomboy

IT DIDN'T TAKE LONG, maybe half an hour, before I fell towhead over tennis shoes in love with Tuolumne Meadows. I had grown to the advanced age of nine with pine trees on the north rim of the Grand Canyon, pine trees on Mount Charleston in Nevada, and scattered ponderosa conifers around the hadn't-quite-made-it resort of Long Barn, California, so it wasn't Tuolumne's forest of scaly-barked lodgepole pines that seduced me. It was more, much more. Awe, soon metamorphosed into love, was inspired by a combination of splendors. It was felt in the cool July breeze; seen in the expansive, river-cut meadows and the domes thrusting boldly into the high blue sky; heard in the sound of rushing water, bird-cry, and breeze; and scented in the pine-needled magic of the Sierra.

My mother, Alice Sargent, my five-year-old sister, Rosalie, and I had just arrived in a camp occupied by several families of Bureau of Public Roads (BPR) engineers, including my dad, Bob Sargent. Friendly women welcomed mother while children inspected us younger interlopers. "The elevation is 8,600 feet here," a woman told mother. "You may want to have your girls rest a while to get used to it."

Simultaneously, but far more quietly, a teenage boy addressed me: "Wanta climb Lembert Dome? Come on." We strolled off, then accelerated as mother called, "Shirley, come back here!" a refrain I was to hear repeatedly during the enchanted summers of 1936 and 1937, summers that merge into one in memory.

Instead of resting on a cot in a tent, I acclimatized myself by scrambling up a steep trail and climbing a granite ridge to the top of Lembert Dome, several hundred feet above the meadows. My leader, Glendon, was offhand when I tried to articulate my wonder at the view, but he pointed out the singular grandeur of Cathedral and

Unicorn peaks to the southwest and Mount Dana, Mount Gibbs, and Mammoth Peak to the east. My lifelong love affair with Tuolumne Meadows—with all of Yosemite National Park—had begun.

What is still remembered as the Great Depression, and the government's efforts to put thousands of men back to work by allocating millions of dollars for highway and bridge construction in National Parks, Forests, and Monuments, was responsible for our being in the high heaven of Tuolumne Meadows. The BPR staff were present, surveying and inspecting the construction progress on a modern highway to replace the narrow, wandering pioneer Tioga Road. My handsome engineer dad was participating in making Yosemite history at the same time as he was keeping his family in beans and bread.

Our BPR camp was already historic—for the irregular rows of tent frames and such amenities as a bathhouse and grease rack that had been built and occupied by the Civilian Conservation Corps (CCC) boys earlier in the thirties—and would later become a summer home for entomologists and various ranger-naturalists. Only the messhall's L-shaped floor was left, but it had been recycled into a platform for Saturday night dances. My parents and other BPR couples circled it, accompanied by band music from car radios. Headlights supplied lighting. Camp kids—there were four or five of us besides the teenager—utilized the flooring for less romantic but eminently satisfactory pursuits such as hopping, jumping rope, and playing with toy cars.

Besides the camp and another larger one a couple of miles to the southwest, the CCC men had constructed the 300-site Tuolumne Meadows campground, which featured granite-rocked, shake-roofed restrooms with inside plumbing—grandeur in the wilds. Our camp had outhouses, but the elegant bathhouse with showers and laundry tubs gave great comfort to cleanliness-minded adults.

Seymour Coffman was resident engineer of the job. His wife soon allied with mother, and their little girl and my sister became inseparable. Glendon's parents were Georgie and Frank Swan. A childless couple named Jack and Pat Kiefer impressed me because they drove clear to Bishop for Sunday Mass. "Fibber" Kenny and his parents, Mary and Lee Storch, and the three Ciceros, were the people I remember best. I'll never forget Carmen Cicero because her exuberant yodels resounded and echoed beautifully through the camp.

But, instead of yodeling, she screamed in the shower when she found the missing and mourned diamond from Mrs. Kiefer's wedding ring. "All the women came running," Carmen recalled, "and Pat nearly fainted. When Jack came home, he was so thankful he drove the long, twisty miles to Lee Vining and bought me a case of beer."

The public campground, constructed in anticipation of an increase in visitation once the new road was finished, had opened barely a month before we arrived. Campers were entertained at night by campfire programs put on by an ardent and popular young ranger-naturalist named Carl Sharsmith. It would be pleasant to say that, at

Steam shovels were still a major piece of road-building equipment in the 1930s. This one was on the new Tioga Road. (YRL Collection)

It didn't take long to fall in love with Tuolumne Meadows. Cathedral Peak is at the left. (YRL Collection)

age nine, I fell under his influence, as I did years later—but not in 1936. However, I had my first lessons in conservation that summer. My "teacher" was not a naturalist but a ranger on the protective staff, then in charge of the Tuolumne Meadows District. His name was Duane Jacobs, and he epitomized the public image of a ranger: tall, handsome, broad-shouldered, quiet-spoken, yet commanding.

I first saw him the morning after we moved into our tent, when he informed Mom why we couldn't keep our cat at Tuolumne. Cats, he said politely, were disruptive if not fatal to wildlife. Our tail-swishing Persian was already on a leash, but mom promised to cage her and send her off via Greyhound bus as soon as possible. My petless aunt and uncle in the desert town of Palmdale agreed to provide her with temporary refuge.

My next encounter with ranger Jacobs was more personal. Dad had made me a slingshot, and I was off in the woods, ineffectually aiming pebbles at a chattering crested jay that, the ranger must have realized, was absolutely safe. Nevertheless, he introduced me to the idea of the fragility of birds and small mammals, for we were being scolded by what I knew as a "picket pin," but which he identified as a Belding ground squirrel.

"Wouldn't it be a shame," he concluded, "if you hurt or killed that pretty bird?"

Not once had he raised his voice or suggested confiscating my weapon, but he left me imbued with a protective zeal that sent me running up the trail onto the granite backbone of Lembert Dome. There, winded but still purposeful, I flung my slingshot off into space—and was immediately sorry. But a childish grasp of preservation, which later expanded, was implanted in my tomboy self.

Our camp was on a sloping mountainside,

93

between but out of sight of both the old and new Tioga roads. Dad set off to work soon after sunlight slanted through the pines, and Mom spent the days working over our two-burner Coleman stove, washing dishes, or performing myriad mundane tasks. Mom andDad's double bed, bunk beds (mine was the top one), a makeshift closet, and pieces of "Hercules mahogany" furnished the adjoining sleeping tent. Strong wooden powder boxes, originally made by the Hercules Powder Company for storing dynamite, were prized because they could be transformed into cupboards, chests, stools, and even chairs.

At night Dad hoisted our cooler, or bear baffle, high in the air to keep food away from bears. Actually, these animals were rarely in our camp. "You and Rosalie used to go with us," Carmen wrote me, "to see the bears at the garbage dump. Some of them were huge. We had a small bear climb a tree in back of the bathhouse once. But our biggest worry was the mice. The minute we extinguished the gas lantern at night, they were scampering all over."

Our screen-sided, canvas-covered "front" room contained a sink with running water, the Coleman stove, a wood-devouring airtight stove, a wood box that I was supposed to help fill, a picnic table, and more pieces of Hercules mahogany. Rosalie was content with playing dolls inside, but I was happier out of the tent's confines and away from mother's admonitions that the wood box needed filling or the broom needed wielding. After breakfast I would escape to the outhouse, and from there take off for hours of freedom. Carmen remembers me as "always on the go, looking for new places to explore."

Often I perched on top of a steep, triangular-sided boulder just off the shoulder of the new road, carefully writing down the numbers affixed to dump trucks, road graders, and steam shovels. No doubt amused at my industry, drivers would wave. Further delight was supplied by the times when my sister found me but could not climb up to join me.

Since electrification was far in the future, the only item on ice in our camp was beer. Bottles were kept in a snow-filled washtub, replenished a couple of times a week from slow-melting drifts near Tioga Pass. The inviting tub was kept in the shade of pines on the slope above our tent. Anticipating a clandestine tasting session, Dad gave me a bottle to try. A hearty swallow instantly forestalled youthful addiction.

Another recreational feature of camp life was a horseshoe pit near our tent. The clunk and thud of horseshoes were accompanied by masculine shouts of "Anybody can see that's a leaner!" Such comments and spirited arguments coincided with the squeals of whichever delighted youngster was being pushed high in the tire swing by a man awaiting his turn at horseshoes.

On weekdays at least two of the women— Mom being one—drove down to the meadow, where radio reception was clear enough to hear "Stella Dallas" and "Mary Marlin." Rosalie was still so young she took naps, and she would curl up on the back seat. I was supposed to stay in camp, but more likely I was out in the woods or along the Dana Fork of the Tuolumne River, forbidden territory which, Mom warned, "you could drown in." That was possible, but there were many safe places to wade across to the other side. Often I was followed by Fibber Kenny, a six-year-old who loved both to fish and prevaricate.

One time he tagged along and witnessed my tumble into the water. I remember undressing except for my underpants, leaving my clothes on a boulder to dry, and wandering off with Kenny's "wait for me" plaint his sole reaction.

The grass was greener and thicker on the other side of the river. Furthermore there were few observers—perhaps an occasional fisherman or two—whereas there were cars, drivers, and admonitory adults on the camp side. Once, while I was lacing my shoes after a crossing with them held in my hands, one fell in the river and was swept away. Catastrophe! Not only would Mother know that I had disobeyed her, but I had only one other pair of shoes—school shoes. The word "Depression" meant little to me except that we couldn't afford anything extra. That had been brought forcibly home to me after I had carelessly dropped our sole flashlight down an outhouse hole. If flashlights were essential and expensive, then shoes, I realized, must be even more so.

After work, Dad and I hunted for the missing tennis shoe, which, fortunately, he found—thoroughly waterlogged. My parents were neither tyrannical nor penurious, just scraping by on about one hundred dollars a month. "You girls and your mother," Carmen Cicero said, "often went to Lee Vining with us to buy groceries. We *tried* to get by on a dollar a day for food."

My next misadventure in the Dana Fork involved a rock cutting a bare toe. I howled loudly enough so that Carmen alerted Mother: "Alice, I think Shirley is drowning." My Mom's unflappable reply, repeated to me later, was, "She wouldn't be making that much noise if she was drowning." Retribution for that episode was worse than a spanking, for Mom cleaned out the wound with a liberal application of smelly, stinging iodine. Iodine, castor oil, and, it seemed to me, spankings, were Mom's remedies for any and all physical and behavioral problems. Fortunately praise and hugs were also given freely.

Thunder, lightning, and pouring rain were a frequent afternoon diversion. Our tent leaked, and Mom developed a rating system for a storm's severity. A two- or three-pan storm with the

accompanying sound of plunks and drips was easily controllable, but an eight-pan and once even a ten-pan rain overtaxed her supply of utensils. I enjoyed dumping pans into a bucket, and was exhilarated by the fast-moving storms and warmed by the airtight stove and mugs of cocoa.

One memorable day I was caught out in the woods by a storm, and quickly soaked. I frantically sought shelter, and found a small cave somewhere in the vicinity of Puppy Dome. While I shivered, teeth chattering, I glanced around in the gloom, and discerned rude but colorful stick figures—Indian pictographs. I was awed, and planned to bring my family to see them, but I never could relocate the place.

Being sent on an errand to the store down the old road was always a joy. Since Puppy Dome was just across a meadow from the large, long tent that housed food, camping equipment, fishing supplies, and some clothes, a quick climb and a few moments to savor the view from the top prefaced my trip. After buying whatever mother

One of the spectacular views from the summit of Mount Dana is of the Mono Craters to the southeast. (YRL Collection)

needed, I would become mesmerized by a tantalizing display of rubber and leather boots shelved at the back of the store. I had studied them frequently, and had decided on a pair of ankle-high, laced leather boots as essential to my well-being. No other boots, either in the store or in the indispensable wish-books—"Sears 'n Sawbucks" and "Monkey Wards" catalogs—could possibly carry me up to a mountaintop more comfortably and speedily than they.

Of course my parents were acutely aware of my obsession, but when the glad day came that I really was to climb a mountain, I wore my badly worn tennis shoes. New ones had been ordered but had not yet arrived. Glendon, his father, Dad, and I drove to a parking lot near Tioga Pass, then took off across the flowery, somewhat boggy meadow toward Mount Dana, towering above us, red and rocky, at 13,053 feet. The fact that the elevation of Tioga Pass, our starting point, was 9,945 feet did not diminish my exultation: I was going to climb a 13,000-foot peak!

Dad had warned me that I was not to complain, and, though frequently breathless and weary, I didn't. Near the top, however, rocks cut through the sole on one shoe, and I asked him to carry me. "No way" was not a common expression then, but his response was negative. He and the others left me behind. It was so quiet that I could hear water from melting snow gurgling under the jumble of rocks. Slowly, gingerly, I limped after them, trying to keep the torn shoe from touching the sharpest rocks.

By the time I reached the top, the tear and the discomfort had grown considerably, but were instantly dismissed in wonder at the vistas.

Above, the azure sky formed a dazzling arc, encircling me was infinity, and below was color, in green meadows, the blue glints of ponds, and expanses of lakes. Dad pointed out Mono Lake on the east, beyond which, he told me, was high desert and Nevada. He swiveled to point out the familiar dominant peaks to the west: Cathedral. Unicorn, Cockscomb. I identified Lembert Dome, but its stature, hitherto so impressive, seemed reduced.

In that array of beauty and might, amid surroundings of unimaginable natural grandeur, I felt awed, enriched, and humble. In many ways, that climb to the summit of Dana was the high point of my childhood.

When we arrived back at camp I was limping, both shoe soles flapping and a stocking cut through, but still I was exhilarated and inspired. Dad said proudly, "Here's a hiker who deserves a pair of boots." Mom's response was less positive. "Maybe for Christmas, but just look at what came in today's mail." New blue tennis shoes that looked, and felt, wonderful.

12

Yosemite at War

ALTHOUGH Yosemite residents had been virtually untouched by the stringent effects of the Depression, World War II affected them dramatically from beginning to end. Like Americans everywhere, Yosemiteites were outraged to hear the news on December 7, 1941.

Radio reception was always poor in Yosemite Valley, and Pete Hoss remembers "hearing about the Japanese attack on Pearl Harbor over the staticky radio. I could not comprehend much at age seven, but knew from my parents' reaction that it was terrible news."

Bob Wagner, then five, had a similar memory. "My family strained to hear broadcasters' comments over our Philco console, as did I. Whatever was being said, I knew it was awful."

Gas rationing and all-out war efforts, which employed women as well as men, kept the formerly traveling public at home. In 1941 nearly 600,000 people visited the Park. By 1943 visitation was less than 128,000, and the following year below 120,000! Concessionaire revenue was equally depleted, and local manpower—the best, brightest, and youngest—enlisted or were drafted into the armed services.

Within months, Yosemite Elementary alumnus Rusty Rust joined the army, as did Jules Ashworth and Bob and Roy Lally. Herb Ewing and Ev Harwell became pilots in the Army Air Force, Lawrence Merriman, Jr. enlisted in the navy, and Lloyd Kramer was in Naval Intelligence. John Telles, Jr., Burleigh and Jay Johnson, Nick Brochini, and Allen Levine, all from the Indian Village, also served in the military. There were many other servicemen: for example, the Yosemite Park and Curry Company listed seventy-one on a framed honor roll. Only one was a woman: Barbara Van Housen, who enlisted in the newly-organized Women's Army Corps. Della Dondero and Velda Johnson, also WACs, represented the local Indians. Sisters Audrey and Doris Beck enlisted in the WAVES, and Margaret Anne Taylor joined the Marine Corps. Considering the limited population of Yosemite, the number of people in service was impressive. Some did not survive, including Lt. Levine, who was killed in battle.

The Civilian Conservation Corps was an early casualty of the war. Its termination in 1942 provided capable manpower for the armed forces, but an end to the tremendous benefits in improvements and maintenance in many national parks.

Before the post-flood camp was dismantled,

One of the few tangible remains of the CCC is this handsome rock fireplace and chimney. (Photograph by Kaye B. Ferrara)

The U.S. Navy took over The Ahwahnee Hotel early in 1943, and stayed until after World War II ended. (YRL Collection)

Mike Adams and his pals "would sneak in and try to bowl" in the recreation hall. Later all of the buildings were removed, but today a seldom-seen remnant, a handsome rock fireplace and chimney, testifies to the workers' skill and the CCC program.

Several structures in the main Wawona camp were used by Signal Corps units who trained there during the war. Some recycled buildings are still being used by the Park Service.

Another near casualty was the Curry Company itself. By August of 1942, Don Tresidder, convinced that it would not survive, fired many of his employees, including executives, and left only a caretaker staff to serve the ever-declining number of guests.

Pete Hoss has never forgotten that day. "I walked home from school, and my father [Herman Hoss], secretary-treasurer for the Curry Company, told me the company was drastically curtailing operations, and we would be leaving Yosemite. I think we all thought we would live there forever. I had a feeling of emptiness that lasted a long time, but Yosemite through the years of visits and summer jobs is still a second home to me."[1]

---

1. One of the first boys in a Palo Alto school to befriend Pete was Ed Hardy, the Curry Company's president from 1974 to 1993.

Until 1948, the only ski "lifts" at Badger Pass were two barge-like conveyances called Big Bertha and the Queen Mary. (YP & CC Collection)

Beginning in the spring of 1942, two large areas south of the school were dug up and fenced for Victory Gardens. Vegetables were in short supply and "environmental impact" was an unknown term. Even though there was more of a community feeling, and both gardens were in the same general area, they were separate. "To keep deer out, the 'Company' garden was surrounded by rabbit-wire," Stewart Cramer observed, "while the 'Government' garden was protected by an electric fence. At recess we children would form a long line, holding hands, and one of our braver classmates would touch the wire, giving us all a mild-to-medium shock."

Despite the physical separation between the gardens, the twain did meet, according to John Degen, who said, "Our family had two plots, one in the Curry garden, the other in the NPS garden. Both had piped water, and both took a lot of work."

"Taking care of the plots was not very interesting to me," Charlotte Ewing admitted. "Weeding was hot and tiring and our plot wasn't terribly productive, but other people raised green peppers, corn, string beans, and wonderful tomatoes."

Mary Degen recalled that "One year there was a bumper crop of apples in Hutchings' and Lamon's old orchards, so an old-fashioned cider press was brought in, and one Saturday everyone took turns squeezing apples. There were gallons of juice. Some of ours turned hard! The bears got to eat all the left over pulp."

Mike Adams' memory differs only slightly. "We had apple fights, and we squeezed worms and all into delicious juice."

Teachers and parents imbued the children with patriotic fervor, Mary said. "We'd have scrap metal drives and we took our Mom's old pots and pans to school, along with tin foil balls, rubber bands, and empty toothpaste tubes. We girls wore plastic shoes, and hair barrettes shaped like flags and V for Victory lapel pins. The boys wore beanies with a V on the front, and we'd talk about how much we hated Hitler and Tojo."

Before Pete Hoss left the Valley he bought "25¢ stamps to place in War Bond books that said 'Zap the Jap.'" Stewart mentioned another way in which youngsters could help. "For civil defense purposes, our principal was required to make up a list of the older children, including whether or not we had skis or a bicycle, so that we might be called upon as messengers in an emergency."

The bicycle brigade that had escorted President Roosevelt around the Valley was proud to be mobilized. "I was special delivery girl, taking special mail to the Ahwahnee," Charlotte said. "Believe me, I felt very important."

The Park's involvement with the war effort was as unique as its geographical location. As early as 1940, the U.S. Army had stayed in Valley campgrounds. After war was declared, the Signal Corps was at Wawona, and, Stewart said, "Camp 11 (now Upper Pines) became a small army camp. Army units would bivouac here and hike the trail to Vernal and Nevada Falls. With other valley residents, one day, I watched a battalion of troops pass in review after standing a retreat ceremony in the Ahwahnee Meadow."

Both the bear feeding and the firefall had been stopped after Pearl Harbor, but in the spring of 1943, the army commander asked Frank Kittredge, the new park superintendent, for a firefall. Kittredge okayed it, and as Stewart related, "The request was given to the Curry Co. and passed along to my father. I was twelve at the time. Together, we climbed the Four-Mile Trail, still covered with snow at the top, and let ourselves into the boarded-up Mountain House, where we spent the night. The next day we built the fire, and after dark showed the army and everyone else a near record-sized firefall."

No request or directive from Uncle Sam was more startling than an admiral's selection of the Ahwahnee as a convalescent hospital! By June of 1943 the navy had landed, and several hundred displaced sailors were packed into the former luxury hotel. Unlike guests, their appreciation of the surrounding natural grandeur was minimal. In fact, their oft-repeated complaint, "I joined the navy to sail the high seas, not the high Sierra," expressed the common reaction to being shut-in and isolated from entertainment, girls, and beer. In time those lacks would be filled by local people, organizations from the San Joaquin Valley, and sales of beer.

Superintendent Kittredge, who was strongly anti-liquor, allowed an enclosure to be built adjacent to the Old Village Store. "It soon acquired the title of Frank's Place," Stewart remembered. "Customers purchased bottles of beer and ale through a window, and used the benches and patio tables. There was a fence all around, and an outhouse."

Before entertainment was organized, Nancy Loncaric told an audience of sailors, "I think it's awful, the navy put you here," and after cheers, played the piano for them. "I said, 'if any of you want to come to my home and listen to some of my records, you are welcome.' A number of them did just that, and even though some of them had never heard of Chopin, Beethoven, etc., they enjoyed the beautiful music."

Her direction of a Christmas play in 1943 involved the entire student body. "I played Santa Claus," Bob Lake remembered, "and Mary Degen (just about my best friend) played Mrs. Santa. It

The weapons of war were a sharp contrast to the elemental peace of nature. (YRL Collection)

must have turned out pretty well because we took it to the Ahwahnee for wounded sailors and Marines in January. So, we did indeed entertain the troops."

On January 14, the delighted sailors applauded everything from the Rhythm Band's rendition of "Anchors Aweigh," to eight-year-old Anne Adams' piano solo, traditional carols, and the two-act play.

Over the years, Mrs. Loncaric directed many pageants, remembered fondly by the now-adult participants. In 1933, Barbara Degen was "a flower girl in a lavender dress" in a spring pageant held outdoors. May Day was also celebrated outside, with the girls draped in white dresses dancing around a Maypole.

Another May Day ritual remembered by Char-

During the war years, reading, studying, and listening to news of battles on the radio was the evening pastime. Pictured here are Laurie and Jack Degen, Barbara, John, Mary Jane, and a cousin in the living room of their house near the foot of Yosemite Falls. (Mary Degen Rogers Collection)

lotte was the filling of baskets with grasses and maybe pieces of ferns, "not necessarily flower flowers, placing them on neighbors' doorsteps, ringing doorbells, and racing away giggling."

Pete Hoss had good reason to remember the "Frog Prince" play. "Mike Adams, about eight then, was chosen as the Prince. On the day of the play, however, he smoked a cigarette and got sick. I had to take the role."

"One play was about other countries, and we all dressed in appropriate costumes and did a dance," Beverly Wagner recalled. "I was 'Little Olga from across the Volga.'"

After Red Skelton entertained the sailors, Virginia Adams brought him to the school where, teacher Annette Zaepffel said, "He did a 'he bee, she bee' number on the stage."

"His visit was a highlight," according to Jim Wagner. Jim Ouimet added that the comedian was "hilarious. Everything he said made us laugh."

"Families of medical and line officers lived in housekeeping units at Yosemite Lodge and Camp Curry," Stewart explained, "and their children attended Yosemite Elementary and Mariposa High."

"At Y.E.S., we made new friends with the new-comers," Mike Adams added. "If we were lucky, we got invited to see movies in the Navy's recreational hall, a temporary building in the former flower gardens."

Pat Phillips said, "One new girl named Mary Dewgaw could think up outrageously funny things to do. We always thought it was because she was Navy and had *traveled!* None of us had been anywhere, and she was from another state!

"Actually the war was an exciting time for all the kids. At first, there were the soldiers marching on the roads and great entertainment to watch. Then when the Navy took over The Ahwahnee for a hospital there were lots of young men there. We were too young to be interested in men, but a lot of them treated us as they did their brothers or sisters. The flyers were the most fun as they would often come back and fly down the valley very low and sometimes upside down—we always seemed to know when they would be coming although supposedly the government didn't. Of course as an adult I know that they also knew, but as kids we made a great secret of when they would buzz the school. Some of them had been football players in college, so they came and coached the boys in sports, which was very beneficial for the boys."

Both doctors Dewey and Sturm had joined the service, but medical care was provided by navy doctors. After the head nurse left, Pat's mother, Claire Phillips, confessed that she was an R.N. Her employment precipitated a squabble reflecting the lingering NPS/Curry schism.

"As head nurse, doing everything including assisting with surgeries, Mom had to have a telephone and they were hard to get," Pat recorded. "The government agreed to her priority, but insisted that because she lived in company housing, the telephone would have to be installed outside on a tree! Mom and Dad said that was ridiculous. Finally Frank Ewing, NPS operations manager, got involved, and said the regulations were silly. Even though Dad didn't work for the government, Mom did, had to have a phone, and it had to be inside our house. That ended the bureaucratic nonsense."

Because of the teacher shortage, mothers such as Muriel Ouimet, Dorothy Holmes, and Millie Anderson, who had taught before moving to

Yosemite, pitched in as substitutes. Nine different teachers came and went in the two-teacher school during the four years of the war. Gayle Tarnutzer, who taught the lower grades for a while, is remembered by Bob McIntyre, Jr.

In 1992 he related that fifty years ago, "A foundation of reading and arithmetic skills was given me by the close cooperation of Gayle Tarnutzer, my first-grade teacher, and my mom. Mrs. Tarnutzer also helped expand my awareness of others, punctuated by the first and only paddling I received in school. Ernie, a master craftsman (and custodian) kept my tricycle in top shape for my daily commute across the Valley to school and back.

"I was keenly aware of complicated undercurrents: girls versus boys, Indians versus non-Indians, Yosemite versus Mariposa. It was easier for me to handle the challenges of natural wilderness than the seemingly wilder and less predictable challenges faced while developing and maintaining relations."

Annette "Zeppie" Zaepffel took over the lower grades in 1943, and particularly recalls the happy time when Red Skelton visited school, and the sad time when ranger's son Donny Hoyt, "a wonderful, lively, bright-eyed little boy," died from a ruptured appendix.

In 1942, Jane T. Wilder was enticed from retirement in Palo Alto to teach the upper grades, which she did until 1949. At first, children such as Luci Richter Clark "thought she was a bear, but she turned out to be dear and charming."

Pat Phillips felt then that Mrs. Wilder was "old, probably in her 60s, but to us old," and a grandmother, imagine! In fact her pretty granddaughter Jane Magee not only lived with her but attended class under her. "I think it must have been hard for Jane," Pat added, "as I don't remember that we really included her much."

But Mary Degen felt that Mrs. Wilder "was the best teacher I ever had. Very strict, but she sure knew how to teach four grades at once and have

The first Girl Scout troop in Yosemite was led by teacher Gayle Tarnutzer. (Anne Adams Helms Collection)

them remember what she taught."

"I think we felt lucky to have her," Pat agreed. "She really stretched our minds. She had an early variable grade system. If someone had a hard time reading, that person might read with a lower grade. Frequently I did reading or math with the next grade up. It was a good system that allowed a student to progress at a realistic rate, and not be held back because other students weren't ready."

The school's reference room was in a corner stacked high with outdated encyclopedias and

Chief Ranger Townsley's official hat fit loosely on his young son, but John wore one of his own later, as a ranger in Yosemite and as superintendent of Yellowstone National Park until his premature death in 1982. (John Reymann Collection)

visited the Indian camp, but my nurse Mom did, and she used to fuss about the fact that there was a central washhouse, and no bathrooms in their homes."[2] The Indian women respected Mrs. Phillips and liked having her warm and competent assistance during childbirth.

Except for the winter of 1942–43, Badger Pass continued operations, largely because skiing was a recreational bonus for the navy personnel in Yosemite, and for bus loads of men from Castle Army Air Force Base near Merced.

"One of the best parts of winter," Jim Ouimet wrote nostalgically, "was the Wednesday ski lesson or, as it is still known, 'Ski Day.' We stayed in school until about 12:30 and then everyone would get on some of the oldest buses that the Yosemite Park and Curry Company had. The oldest ones were the Whites, which were big and slow and leaked exhaust and oil fumes up through the floor boards. The trip to Badger in one of them was quite an experience when everyone arrived nauseated. The first ski lessons I had weren't much fun. The leather boots had no insulation, and after about an hour I couldn't feel my feet. From there, the cold worked up over my whole body. I looked forward to the *end* of the lesson so I could go into the lodge and get a candy bar or hot chocolate. On the trip back to the Valley, I would be in pain as my feet began to thaw out. When I was in the seventh and eighth grades, the ski lessons became the highlight of the winter. By this point, we had all graduated from the advanced classes and the ski instructors had to find challenges for us. I can remember skiing with Nic Fiore where we would play follow the leader down the mountain trying to find the most difficult terrain."

National Geographics. A one-room county library in the Park museum was frequently visited by Pat Phillips and Pat Deane, who were determined to "read every book in the library. No TV then and books were wonderful entertainment." Football diminished her brother Ted's time, but not interest, in reading.

"We went to school with the resident Indians, and I don't remember any discrimination," Pat reflected. "I really liked Charlie Castro. I never

---

2. By 1960 the few remaining Indians were integrated with other Valley residents, and the small village was eradicated.

Football games—and losses—continued, too. Anne Adams challenged the system when, "As an early feminist (or tomboy), I talked my way onto the football team and was promptly tackled by some big guy and broke my wrist."

Anne belonged to the Girl Scouts, but organization of a troop for boys did not appeal to them, according to her brother Mike. "We resisted for several years, saying that we did everything that Boy Scouts did and more since we lived in Yosemite."

Among favorite activities for Mike and his adventuresome pals was "building a flat-bottomed scow and trying it out on the Merced River early in the morning. Boating was not allowed, so if they saw us, rangers ran us off."

Rafting, now so popular, was also forbidden, but that didn't stop the boys. "In spring, we would build rafts in the woods near the base of Yosemite Falls, then launch them on Yosemite Creek, and float (really pole them across rocks and sandbars). Once on the river, we could float down as far as El Capitan Meadow."

Even more exciting were the heavy winters when the boys cut large slabs of ice near the housekeeping camp, "and floated down the river until they broke up near Old Village."

Rock climbing behind the old Yosemite Lodge was yet another pursuit. "The rangers would make us come down for not registering with the Park Service, and creating a traffic jam when visitors stopped to observe us rappelling down."

Class pictures, this one of fifth through eighth graders in 1944–45, were taken yearly. Front row, left to right: George Murphy, Mike Adams, Larry Hoyt, Ted Phillips, Joe Rhoan, Paul dePhyffer, and Pete Robinson sticking out his tongue because he didn't want his picture taken! Middle row: Joan Wosky, Katherine Cramer, Donna Alexander, Anne Adams, Joan VanHousen, Beverley Wagner, Doris Hewitson, and Pat Robinson. Back row: Bob Lake, Bill Godfrey, Stewart Cramer, Dick Klein, Hazel Cramer, Mary Degen, LaVerne Cuthbert, and Jane Magee. (Mary Degen Rogers Collection)

Both the boys and the girls hiked. Ascending Half Dome was almost obligatory. Swimming in the frigid Merced was the summer pastime. "We could swim like fish," Pat said. "When we grew older, we would take air mattresses and float on the river. That was years before rafts were rented. Red Cross lessons were given at the Lodge pool and I took them sometimes."

When polio was rampant, Pat quit swimming because her parents felt that "crowds and water somehow spread the virus. I think our healthy life and not having close contact with the crowds in the Valley was a help. Only one child in the Park contracted polio that I know of, and that was Randy Rust who had a light case."

Pat did not follow her mother's profession of nursing, but Mary Degen and Roberta Castro did. Mike Adams was disinterested in becoming a photographer like his famous father, and became a doctor. Anne worked in Best's Studio as a teenager, and eventually became a business-woman as well as a mother.

Virginia and Ansel gave "wonderful parties and had all those creative people from San Francisco. My parents were always invited," Pat said. The town/gown syndrome was still alive, but couples such as the Adamses and Sturms neither believed in nor perpetuated it.

Time, not the war, diminished the band of pioneers. Bridget Degnan died in 1940, her husband, John, in 1943. During that same year, Mabel Boysen, and consequently Boysen's Studio, expired, and Chief Ranger Forest Townsley had a fatal heart attack near a high-country lake that already bore his name. His sixteen-year-old son John, born and raised in the Park, had to move away with his mother, but returned within a few years as a ranger. Mary Ellen Degnan, aided by nieces and nephews, took over the family business; later, her doctor-brother John was also actively involved. Only Rose and Gabriel Sovulewski and Forest Townsley were allowed to be buried in the Valley's pioneer cemetery; more graves for school children to decorate on Memorial Day. Townsley's death impressed them, for they had known him as a figure of authority all their lives.

One of the better wartime memories Elton Murphy recalled was of the time an ace Navy pilot, who had shot down twenty-one Japanese planes, visited school. Everyone from the youngest boys to Ernie Collins, the custodian, was impressed.

In 1944, Yosemite households received static-plagued radio broadcasts of the agonizing details of the allied invasion of Europe, and the tenacious battles in the Pacific. World War II was winding down, signalling both the Park Service and the Curry Company to plan ahead to normalcy after gas rationing ceased and travel increased.

V-E Day, signifying Victory in Europe, was anticipated and rumored during the spring of 1945. Stewart remembers the April day "when a well-meaning lady bustled into school, and informed us dramatically that the war was over! As it turned out, V-E Day didn't take place until May 8, and on that day school was dismissed early."

The celebration was a bit subdued, because fierce fighting in the Pacific continued. It took three more months and two atom bombs to force Japan's surrender on August 15, 1945, V-J Day.

As anticipated, the war's end and the expiration of gas rationing resulted in a surge of visitation that increases yearly, as people sought, and still seek, recreation and re-creation in the vast diversity of Yosemite National Park.

Then as now, growing up in Yosemite was taken for granted by its children. Not many of them truly or completely realized how privileged they had been until they were distant from it. Not all of them could cope with the so-called real world of cities, throngs of people, and job competition after the real world of nature and protected employment with either the government or the concessionaire.

Stewart Cramer acquired some perspective at an early age because of an absence. "A happy event of my childhood—in terms of contrast—was returning to the fourth grade at Yosemite Elementary after a month in a public school in Cleveland, Ohio, a brick building that made me think I was in a penitentiary."

Partly due to parental distress because their adolescents had to take the long bus ride to Mariposa High—off in the dark and home after dark in winter—and partly due to status, numbers of children were sent to private high schools during the 1940s and '50s. Wasatch Academy in Utah was the favorite boarding school. Distance and absence usually resulted in an earlier maturing, and a new perspective for the teenagers on what Yosemite meant to them. Others, such as Anne Adams and Mary Degen, had moments of comprehension that are embedded in earlier memories. "Who else had recess amid such scenery?" Anne asked. "There were very peaceful, happy mornings, with the sun coming through the trees and Yosemite Falls roaring and the Steller's jays squawking. I do think that I was aware that we were privileged to live in such a beauty-filled place."

Mornings were special to Mary, too. "I remember best walking to school on the Lost Arrow footpath. The wildlife I'd see, and the changes of the seasons along Yosemite Creek are unforgettable. In the early spring the ice cone (that built up at the base of the upper fall during winters), would come crashing down and fill the creek, bank to bank, with blocks of ice and snow, even burying the footbridges."

Because I, Shirley Sargent, had lived in so many places before and after my Tuolumne Meadows baptism, I experienced an awed sensitivity when I was nine or ten. For several Sundays I worshipped in a granite floored "church," with a boulder for an altar and silent lodgepole pines for parishioners. At those times I expressed gratitude for my surroundings and my good fortune, my special privilege, at living there. Later, a five-month residence in Yosemite Valley, including a stint at the school, only intensified my appreciation for Yosemite, this beloved place of singular beauty and multiple wonders.

Childhoods of enchantment end only in physical ways—age, size, residence elsewhere, occupation—but endure in abiding memories. Stuart Cross reveals that "My overriding memory is the continuing sense of wonder and awe which still comes on me whenever I visit. This repeated experience, as small as seeing the evening primroses open in Stoneman Meadow, or as large as the view from Taft Point, Washburn Point, or Clouds Rest, is, I think, that common awareness of something beyond ourselves, some particular sensitivity to the natural world that all of us who know Yosemite share."

Sources

Chapter 1, Yosemite Valley Tomboys.

Prime sources were Hutchings' *In the Heart of the Sierras,* 1886; Charles Warren Stoddard's *In the Footprints of the Padres,* 1867; and Therese Yelverton's *Zanita,* 1872. I consulted both the rough draft and the published article, "A Pioneer's Daughter Returns to Yosemite," by Elizabeth H. Godfrey, in the April 1942 *Yosemite Nature Notes.* I also referred to Cosie Hutchings Mills' October 15, 1941 letter to Mrs. Godfrey, "Miss Cozie of the Yosemite" by Harriett Farnsworth, in the Nov.-Dec. 1965 issue of *True West,* and to my own *Pioneers in Petticoats.*

I find that certain Yosemite histories—some old, others new—are indispensable. *In the Heart of the Sierras,* by James M. Hutchings, first published in 1886, although undeniably partisan (e.g., John Muir is never mentioned by name), is a classic. So is Carl P. Russell's *100 Years in Yosemite,* originally published in 1931, but frequently reprinted—most recently in 1992 by the Yosemite Association. At the risk of immodesty, my own *Pioneers in Petticoats* (1966, et. seq.), and *Yosemite and Its Innkeepers* (1975, still in print) are good sources, as are Hank Johnston's two-volume *Yosemite Yesterdays* (1988 and 1991), which deal with numerous subjects in depth. Al Runte's *Yosemite, The Embattled Wilderness* gives broad coverage to environmental experimentation. Francis P. Farquhar's classic *Place Names of the High Sierra* was a 'bible.' Now the new and greatly expanded *Yosemite Place Names* by Peter Browning (Great West Books, 1988) serves in its place. Although plagued with errors, Linda K. Greene's three-volume *Historic Resource Study* of Yosemite, published by the National Park Service in 1987, is a monumental resource. So is *Tradition and Innovation: A Basket History of the Indians of the Yosemite-Mono Lake Area,* by Craig D. Bates and Martha J. Lee, published by the Yosemite Association in 1990.

Chapter 2, Camping in Yosemite.

The major source was the journal of Alice Chase Dudley. Other than that, I studied *In the Heart of the Sierras* by Hutchings, researched the hotel register for Dudley's Station at the Mariposa County Historical Society, and referred to early references on the Yosemite Valley Chapel. I also had a number of consultations with George Mc-Lean, Alice Dudley's grandson.

Chapter 3, Yosemite School Days

Larry V. Degnan's letters, and his articles: "The Yosemite School," in the February, March, April, and May 1956 issues of *Yosemite Nature Notes;* and "Herzog's Painting of the Cosmopolitan Saloon," in the July 1954 issue. I have also quoted from Dr. John P. Degnan's article, "A Winter Night in Yosemite," in *Yosemite—Saga of a Century, 1864–1964,* published by the Sierra Star Press in 1964. Additionally, I consulted the July 6, 1952 interview of Larry V. Degnan by Dorothy Holmes in the *Fresno Bee,* and the August 3, 1960 interview of Mary Ellen Degnan by Karl Kidder in the *Bee.* My own letters to Larry Degnan and several of his to me, preserved in the Yosemite Research Library, were also helpful, as was the December 1934 statement by Bridget and John Degnan, and a brief December 1941 memoir by Mary Ellen Degnan.

Chapter 4, Wawona Boyhood, 1884–1900.

Background information exists in the Bruce Family Bible, the *Mariposa Gazette* for February 25, 1911, the *Mariposa Gazette Centennial Edition,* 1954, a December 30, 1961 letter from Harriet Bruce Harris, "Reminiscences" of Charlotte Bruce Gibner, and Jay Cook Bruce's book, *Cougar Killer.* My thanks go to Roberta Bruce Phillips for her assistance.

Chapter 5, Childhood of Enchantment, 1894–1910.

Marjorie Cook Wilson's autobiographical manuscript was my chief source for information and quotation. Other official documentation was found in the 1910 census enumeration for Yosemite Valley, the December 10, 1910 death certificate for J. B. Cook, the inquest file, the Mariposa County Probate Court records for Cook, and Cook's will, dated June 29, 1904. Additional information was obtained from the 1903–1912 correspondence file for the Sentinel Hotel, *Mariposa Gazette* news items, the *Merced Sun* of December 27, 1910, dates given me by Wawona Washburn Hartwig, and an April 1965 interview with Dorothy Atkinson's widowed husband, Leonard Bardsley.

Chapter 6, Village Youths.

Although my February 13, 1992 interview with Virginia Best Adams was my chief source for information on her childhood, I also consulted almost daily letters exchanged between Anne and Henry Best in April and May 1905, the *Mariposa Gazette* 1901–1905, the January 1914 *Out West*, "Best's Studio" by Virginia Best Adams in *Saga of a Century*, Sierra Star Press, 1964, and the *Mariposa Gazette Centennial Edition*, 1954.

Thanks to the generosity of Ranger-Interpreter Steve Harrison, who began research on Arthur C. Pillsbury while stationed in Yosemite, I was able to assemble information on his adopted children. Quotations are from letters written by Grace Pillsbury to Steve in 1978, and letters between 1978 and 1985 and a narrative titled "Uncle" by Arthur F. Pillsbury, which were lent to me by Steve.

As indicated in my text, Hart and Beth Cook's book, *My Mother the Chef*, gave me details of Hart's Yosemite adventures. Material on the Sovulewski family was unearthed in the Yosemite Research Library, including taped interviews with Tom Sovulewski by Gene Rose in 1988, and Everett Harwell in October 1992. Letters from Nancy Taylor Maynard and Margaret Anne Taylor Hanly, information given me by Charlotte Ewing, and the author's own memories of their remarkable mothers and Aunt Gabe were also of aid. Robert Pavlik's article, "The Hutchings-Sovulewski Homesite, 1864–1936," in the

Yosemite Association's Fall 1988 issue provided excellent background material.

Chapter 7, In the Footsteps of John Muir.

Besides Strent Hanna's journal, I consulted Muir's *My First Summer in the Sierra*, Jean Hanna Clark's introduction to *Dear Papa, Letters Between John Muir and His Daughter Wanda*, edited by Clark and Sargent, and "The Sierra Club Outing of 1919," in the *Sierra Club Bulletin* for January 1920.

Chapter 8, The 1920s.

I consulted the basic Yosemite histories that are mentioned elsewhere in these pages, and I solicited contributions from former Yosemite "kids": Virginia Best Adams, Bob Wilkinson, Audrey Beck Wilson, Wawona Washburn Hartwig, Kenneth J. Carpenter, Dorothy Gallison Sprague, Phyllis Freeland Broyles, and John Reymann—all were generous with their special memories. Dorothy Jones Mole and Betty Haigh Keller, who spent most of their childhood summers in Yosemite Valley, added their experiences. I am indebted as well to one 'Don Blank,' who asked to be anonymous.

Chapter 9, A Decade of Changes.

For much of the information on Indians I used "The Yosemite Indian Story," an unpublished manuscript by Ranger Naturalist Harold E. Perry, Sr., in the Yosemite Research Library. This document gives the administrative view, not that of the Indians. The diversity of chapters 9 and 10 was made possible by aid from Virginia Best Adams, Michael Adams, Stewart Cramer, Mary Degen Rogers, Audrey Beck Wilson, Darrol Born, Phyllis Cole Brownell, Everett Harwell, Jane Mc-Kown Chapman, Suzanne McKown Turnquist, Bob McCabe, Lloyd Kramer, Bob Skakel, Pat Oliver, Pat Phillips Kessler, Kenneth Carpenter, John Reymann, Al Gordon, Della Taylor Hoss, Nancy Loncaric, Dick Otter, Charlotte Ewing, Phyllis Reinhart, Bette Waddington, Pete Hoss, Lawrence J. Merriman, Jr., John Merriman, Charles Castro, Jay Johnson, Ralph Parker, Rich Hodges, Jane Trabucco Rust, Randy Rust, Ed Hardy, and Hank Johnston. Surviving copies of the Yosemite Journal and the Mariposa High

School Yearbooks for 1936 through 1939 supplied background information on Leroy "Rusty" Rust.

Chapter 10, The Great Flood.

Many of the names listed for chapter 9 apply to this chapter as well. Documentation for the disastrous flood was in the Superintendent's Monthly Report for December 1937, and Russell L. McKown's report for the same month. I checked the surviving issues of the *Yosemite Residenter* and the *Yosemite Journal*, John Bingaman's *The Ahwahneechees,* and the fine book, *Traditions and Innovations, A Basket History of the Yosemite Indians,* by Craig Bates and Martha J. Lee.

Chapter 11, Tuolumne Tomboy.

My fond and vivid memories were my chief source, backed up by those of Carmen Cicero, an old friend. Records of the Civilian Conservation Corps in the Yosemite Research Library were helpful, as were Linda Greene's *Historic Resource Study*, volumes 2 and 3, and Elizabeth O'Neill's *Meadow in the Sky.*

Chapter 12, Yosemite at War.

Once again I am indebted to many generous people: Peter Hoss, James Wagner, Della Dondero Hern, Michael Adams, Charlotte Ewing, Stewart Cramer, John Degen, Mary Degen Rogers, Nancy Loncaric, Robert Lake, Anne Adams Helms, Beverly Wagner Riddle, Annette Zaepffel, James Ouimet, Pat Phillips Kessler, Robert McIntyre, Jr., Virginia Best Adams, and Stuart G. Cross. All of them shared their unique memories with me. I also consulted copies of the *Ahwahnee News* (mimeographed by the U.S. Naval Hospital) for May 14 and August 14, 1945, and the issues of the *Yosemite Sentinel* for December 25, 1943 and June 18 and August 24, 1945.

Index

*(Numbers in **boldface** refer to photographs.)*

A

Adair, Mary E., **12**
Adams, Anne, 100, 103, **104,** 105
Adams, Ansel, 39, 89, 105
Adams, Gladys, 77
Adams, Mike, 78, 97, 99, 101, **104**–105
Adams, Virginia Best, 78, 89, 101, 105
Agassiz Column, 54–**55**
Ah Mow, 26, 31
Ah Toy, 26
Ah Wong, 26
Ah You, 33
Ahwahnee Hotel, The, 11, 14, 61, **98**
    construction of, 63, 88–89, 100, 101
Alexander, Fred, 43–44
Alexander, June, 62, **77**
All-Year Highway, 57, 59, 61, 84
Amos, Joe, 20–22
Anderson, George G., 5
Anderson, Millie, 74, 101
Ansel Adams Gallery, 44, 58
Ash Can Alley, 63
Ashworth, Jules, 97
Atkinson, Charles, 30, 33
Atkinson, Dorothy, 29–30, 32–33, 35
Atkinson, Nellie, 7, 30

B

Bachagalupi, John Babtiste, 34
Badger Pass Ski Area, 78, 80, 88, **99,**
    103, 105
Barnard's Hotel, 6, 9–10, 12
Barnard, Effie Crippen, 6
Barnard, John K., 5, 11, 16, 17
Barnett, Jim, 68
Bear feeding, 65
Beck, Audrey, 61, 83, 97
Beck, Doris, 97
Bell, Miss, 74
Benny, Jack, 87
Benson, Major H. C., 33
Best's Studio, 35–36, 40, 44, 58, 105
Best, Anne Rippey, 35–36, 38–40
Best, Harry C., 35–36, 38–39, **40,** 41,
    58, 63

Best, Virginia, **35**–36, 37–**40,** 57–58
    See also Adams, Virginia Best
Bierstadt, Albert, 8
Big Oak Flat Road, 5, 41, 48, 55, 70
Big Tree Lodge, 70
Big Tree Room, 6, 25
Black's Hotel, 4, 10, 13, 16
Black, Alex, 4
Blank, Don, 61
Boring, Ora, 38
Born, Darrol, 80, 89
Bow, Clara, 61
Bower Cave, 48
Boysen's Studio, 36, 58, 105
Boysen, Daniel, 36
Boysen, Ellen, **31, 37,** 38, 40–41
Boysen, Mabel, 36, 105
Bracebridge Dinner, 89
Brown, Chris, (Chief Lemee), 58–59,
    60, 72, **73,** 77
Brown, John, 38
Brown, Lena, 38, 58
Brown, Patti, 88
Broyles, Rod, 69
Bruce, Albert Henry, 20
Bruce, Albert O., 20–21, 24
Bruce, Azelia V., 20
Bruce, Bert, 20–22
Bruce, Edward, 21
Bruce, Harriet, 21
Bruce, Jay Cook, 20–23, 43
Bruce, Robert, 21
Bruce, William, 21
Bureau of Public Roads (BPR), 70, 91

C

Camp Ahwahnee, 34, 78
Camp Curry, 11, 17, 18, 25, 54, 58
    children at, 67, **68,** 69
    entertainment at, 63, 75, 77, 78, 84, 89
Camp Lost Arrow, 34
Camp Yosemite, 34, 49
Carpenter, E. T. "Carp", 60
Carpenter, Ken, 60, 62, 90
Carquinez Strait, 47
Carr, Eleanor, **74, 76**
Castro, Charlie, **71,** 75, 77–78, 82, 103
Castro, Roberta, 105
Cavagnaro, Angelo, 15

Cedar Cottage, 25, 42–43, 82
Chadwick's camp, 9
Chadwick, Katy, 8–10
Chowchilla Mountain Road, 20
Cicero, Carmen, 92, 94–95
Civilian Conservation Corps (CCC),
    44, 70–71, 81, 83, **85, 86,** 91, 97–98
Clark, Galen, 3, 5, 8, 14, 17, 20, 29–30
    funeral of, **31**
Clark, Jean Hanna, 46
Clark, Luci Richter, 102
Coffman & Kenney, 14
Coffman, Seymour, 92
Coffman, William F., 16
Colby, Will, 51–53
Cole, Phyllis, 89
Collins, Ernie, 76–77, 102, 105
Conness, Mount, **53**
Conway, John, 9
Cook, Beth, 42
Cook, Ellen C., 42–43
Cook, Fannie, 20, 24, 27, 29
Cook, Hart, Jr., 42–44, 62
Cook, Jay Bruce, 24–25, 27, 29–30,
    33–34, 36
Cook, John J., 20, 24
Cook, Marjorie, 24–27, **29**–30, 32–35, 38
Cook, May C., 24
Coulter, George W., 5
Coulterville, 8, 11, 15, 31, 48
Coulterville Road, 5, 8, 48, 67
Cramer, Helen, 89
Cramer, Sterling S., 78, 84, 89
Cramer, Stewart, 71–72, 78–80, 82–83,
    88–**89,** 99, **104,** 105
Crocker's Station, 56
Crockett, 47, 56
Cross, Stuart, 67–69, 106
Crown Prince of Sweden, 61
Curry Company,
    See Yosemite Park and Curry Co.
Curry, David A., 17, 67
Curry, Foster, 67, 69
Curry, Jennie, 67
Curry, Marjorie, 67, 69
Curry, Mary, 67, 69

D

Dana, Mount, 95–96

Danner, Carl, 90
Deane, Pat, **103**
Degen family, **101**
Degen, Barbara, 100, **101**
Degen, John, 79, 99, **101**
Degen, Mary Jane, 74, 75, 76, 82, 85, 86,
     90, 99, 100, **101**, 102, **104**, 105
Degnan's, 40, 60, 83
Degnan, Alfred, 15, 19
Degnan, Alice, 15, 19, **31**, 38, 41
Degnan, Bridget, **13**, 14–15, 18–19,
     41, 105
Degnan, Chris, 15, 19, 41
Degnan, Daisy, 15
Degnan, John, **13,** 14–15, 17, 19, **31,** 38,
     41, 105
Degnan, John Paul, 15, 19, 105
Degnan, Laurence, 11–12, **13,** 14–18
Degnan, Mary Ellen, 15–16, 18–19, 105
Degnan, Ruth, 15, 19, 38, 41
Del Portal Hotel, 36, 42
Delaney Creek, 50
Dennison, Walter, 15
dePfyffer, Paul, 78, **104**
Desmond Park Service Company, 38,
     41, 60
Dewey, Dr. Hartley, 86, 101
Dewgaw, Mary, 101
Dexter, Kitty, 38
Dick, Sally Ann, 27
Dog Lake, 50
Dondero, Carl, **71**
Dondero, Della, **67,** 82, 97
Dondero, John, **67**
Dudley's Ranch, 8
Dudley, Alice Chase, 7, **8,** 9–10
Dudley, Clara, 8
Dudley, Fannie, 8
Dudley, Hosea, 8
Dudley, Walter Hosea, 8

E
Edison, Thomas, 8
Edris, Ramses, 68
El Portal, 33, 36, 40–41, 43, 77
Eleven-Mile Trail, 54–55
Elk, **64**–67
Ewing, Charlotte, 45, **74,** 87, 89, 100
Ewing, Frank, 44, 101
Ewing, Herb, 45, 89, 97

F
Fairbanks, Doug, 61
Fiore, Nic, 103
Firefall, 7, 17, 69, 99–100
Fiske, George, 29–30, **31**
Fitzpatrick, "Fitz", 81

Foley's Studio, 58
Foley, D. J., 36
Forsyth, Dorothy, 38
Forsyth, Major W. W., 38
Four-Mile Trail, 9, 17, 54, 78, 100
Francisco, 27
Freeland, Phyllis, 69

G
Gallison, Arthur, 62
Gallison, Bob, 62, 65, 84
Gallison, Dorothy, 62
Gallison, Glenn, 62
Garrett, Billie, **37,** 38, 40
Girl Scouts, 102, 104
Glacier Point Hotel, 34, 54, 88
Glasscock, Albert, 25
Goldsworthy, George, 44
Gordon, Al, 81
Gordon, Gladys, 81
Grant, U. S., 12
Green, Rufus, 68

H
Haigh, Betty, 65, 72
Half Dome
     first ascent of, 5
Hall, Ansel, 39
Hall, Frances M., 16
Hanna, David, 46
Hanna, Edna Sheriden, 46
Hanna, Jim, 46
Hanna, John Muir, 46, **47,** 48–54, 56
Hanna, Strentzel, 46–48, **49,** 50–54, 56
Hanna, Susan, 46
Hanna, Thomas Rea, 46
Hanna, Wanda Muir, 46
Hardy, Ed, 98
Harwell, Bert, 69, 78
Harwell, Everett, 64, 74, 89–90, 97
Hazel Green, 48
Hicks, Maud, 74
Hill, Estella, 21
Hill, Thomas, 8, 21–23
     studio of, 7, 21–22
Hilliard, Pete, 43, **70**
Hodges, Clara M., 42
Hodges, Rich, 76, 88
Hoffman, Betty, 80
Holmes, Dorothy, 101
Hood, Glenn, 68
Hooley, Bart, 78, 86
Hooley, Nancy, 78, 86
Hoover, Herbert, 61
Hoss, Della Taylor, 78, 84
Hoss, Herman, 89, 98
Hoss, Pete, 78, 80, 85, 97–98, 101

Howard, Maggie, (Tabuce), **72**–73, 77
Hoyt, Donny, 102
Hutchings cabin, 5, 43
Hutchings House, 1, 4
Hutchings, Augusta, 5–6
Hutchings, Elvira S., 1–2, 4
Hutchings, Florence, **1**–7
Hutchings, Gertrude (Cosie), 3–5, 7,
     18, 22
Hutchings, James Mason, 1–2, **3,** 4–8, 38
Hutchings, William Mason, **3,** 7

I
Indian Field Days, 37, 41
Indian Village, 71, 77
Indians, 12, 20–22, 27, 38, 41, 43, 58, 62,
     67, 71–72, 97, 102
     See also Native Americans
Ivy Cottage, 25–26, 34

J
Jacobs, Duane, 90, 93
Jacobs, Edith, 16
Jacobs, Nola June, **74,** 90
James, Alice, 38
Jewett, Edna, **59**
Jewett, Ruth, **59**
Jilson, Mrs., 68
Jobe, Joe, **59**
Johnson, Jay, 71, 82
Johnson, Velda, **70, 79,** 97
Johnston, Hank, 36
Jones, Dorothy, 59
Jones, Edwin, 59
Jorgensen, Angela Ghirardelli, 29–30
Jorgensen, Chris, 30, 38, 58
Jorgensen, Virgil, 38

K
Kalpine, 12
Kenney, Charley, 17
Kenney, George W., 14, 16
Kenneyville, **14,** 15, 34
Kiddie Kamp, 66–**68**
Kiefer, Jack, 92
Kiefer, Pat, 92
King Albert of Belgium, 61
Kittredge, Frank, 99
Knoblock, Lenore, 74, **79**
Knowles family, 60
Knowles, Sally, **79**
Kramer, Lloyd, 80, 86–87, 97

L
La Casa Nevada
     See Snow's Hotel
La Grange, 48

Lake, Bob, 100, **104**
Lally, Bob, 97
Lally, Catherine, 64, 80
Lally, Roy, 97
Lamon, James, 2, 11
Lancisco, 27
Lane, Emily, 68
Lane, Nell, 68
Lane, Roger, 68
Lasky, Natalie, 68
LeConte Memorial Lodge, 18, 38, 79
Ledge Trail, 6
Lee Hung (Homer Lee), 60
Lee Vining, 92, 95
Leidig's Hotel, 4, **9,** 11, 13, 16, 78
Leidig, Agnes, 11
Leidig, Alice, 13
Leidig, Belle, 13
Leidig, Charles T., 3, 11, 12, 13, 31, 32
Leidig, Don, 13
Leidig, Emma, 13
Leidig, Fred, 4, 11
Leidig, Fred, Jr., 13
Leidig, George F., Jr., 11–12
Leidig, Hulda, 13
Leidig, Isabella, 4, 11–12
Leidig, Jack, 11–13, 76
Leidig, June, 13
Leidig, Kate, 13
Lembert Dome, 50–51, 91, 93
Lemee, Chief
    See Brown, Chris
Leonard, Archie, 13, 31–32
Levine, Allen, 97
Lincoln, Abraham, 20
Lintott, Billy, 60, **79**
Lintott, Bobby, 60
Locust Cottage, 25–26
Loncaric, John, 74
Loncaric, Nancy, 74–75, 100
Lower Village, 4–5, 29

M
Magee, Jane, 102, **104**
Marconi, Guglielmo, 61
Mariposa, 78
Mariposa Battalion, 59
Mariposa Big Tree Grove, 20
Mariposa County Supervisors, 78
Mariposa Grove Museum, 70
Mariposa Grove of Big Trees, 3, 26, 33
Mariposa High School, 57, 60, 78, 81,
    101
Marshall, Robert B., 50
Mather, Stephen T., 51–52
Matthes, François, 19, 40, 47, 50, 52, 53
McCabe, Bob, 73

McCain, B. H. (Bike), 81
McCain, Joanne, 81
McCain, Pat, 81
McCauley, Fred, 17
McCauley, James, 9, 17
McCauley, John, 17
McIntyre, Bob, Jr., 102
McKown, Jane, 74, **76,** 82
McKown, Suzanne, **74,** 82, 89
McPeak, Billy, **59**
Merriman, John "Duke", 74
Merriman, Lawrence, Jr., 81, 97
Merriman, Lawrence, Sr., 81
Michael, Charlie, 40, 69
Michael, Enid, 40, 69
Mist Trail, 10
Mix, Tom, 61
Modesto, 47
Mountain House, **16,** 54, 100
Muir, John, 4, 8–9, 13, 17, 31–33, **46,**
    50–51, 56
Muldoon, Jack, **59,** 66
Murphy, A. J., 5
Murphy, Beatrice, **59**
Murphy, Elton, 105
Murphy, Lizzie, 29
Muybridge, Eadweard, 2

N
Native Americans, 27, 59, 63, 71
    See also Indians
North, Marvin, 79

O
Oak Cottage, 25
Old Mary, 27, 38
Old Village, 49, 58, 60, 62, 65, 82, 104
Old Village Store, 83–84, 88, 100
Oliver, Pat, 90
Oliver, Virginia, 78
Otter, Dick, 77–78
Ouimet, Jim, 101, 103
Ouimet, Muriel, 101

P
Parker, Ralph, **70,** 84
Parks, Harlow, **31**
Parks, Lillian, **31**
Parsons Memorial Lodge, **52**
Patterson, Jack, 83
Pavilion, the, 60, 84
Phillips, Claire, 101
Phillips, Pat, 90, 101–102, 105
Phillips, Pike, 16, 22
Phillips, Ted, 90, **104**
Pickford, Mary, 61
Pillsbury's Studio, 40, 58

Pillsbury, Aetheline, 40, 58
Pillsbury, Arthur, **37, 39,** 40–41, 58
Pillsbury, Arthur C., **40–41,** 58, 63
Pillsbury, Ernest, **37, 39,** 40–41, 58
Pillsbury, Grace, **37, 39,** 40–41, 58
Pioneer History Center, 19
Premier of Greece, 61
Putnam and Valentine, 35–36

R
Randall, Harry, 4
Rangers Club, 88
Raymond, 19, 22
Raymond-Whitcomb tours, 36
Register Rock, 10
Reinhart, Phyllis, 78
Reymann, Bill, 66
Reymann, John, **63,** 66, 71, 90
River Cottage, 4, 25–26
Robinson, C. D., 6
Rock Cottage, 4, 25, **26,** 27
Roosevelt, Franklin D., 70, **87,** 99
Roosevelt, Theodore, 13, 30–31,
    32, 33, 37
Russell, Richard, **89**
Rust, Hilda Jeffrey, 64
Rust, Jess, 64
Rust, Leroy (Rusty), 63–**64,** 65, 78–79,
    80, 97
Rust, Randy, 29, 105

S
Salter, Nelson, 34
Sargent, Alice, 91, 93–96
Sargent, Bob, 91, 93–94, 96
Sargent, Rosalie, 90–91, 94
Sargent, Shirley, 90, 91–96, 106
Sault, Bill, 60, 63
Sell, Will, Jr., 34, 42
Sentinel Hotel, 11, 13, 16, 18, **24, 25,**
    30–31, 34, 36, 41–42, 60, 88
Sharsmith, Carl, 92
Sierra Club, 7, 51–53
Signal Corps, 98
Sinning, Adolph, 10
Sinning, Mrs. Adolph, 10
Skakel, Bob, 81–82, 84–85, 90
Skelton, Red, 101–102
Smith, Laura, 7
Snow Creek Trail, 50, 54
Snow, Albert, 4
Snow, Emily, 4
Snow's Hotel, 4, 10
Soapsuds Row, 62, 64
Solinsky, Donna, 42, **54**
Sonn, Herbert, 69
Southern Pacific Railroad, 17

Sovulewski, Bob, 42–43
Sovulewski, Gabriel, 34, 38, 43, 105
Sovulewski, Gabrielle, 42–**44,** 53, **54**
Sovulewski, Grace, **31,** 38, 43–44
Sovulewski, Joe, 42–43
Sovulewski, Lawrence, 43
Sovulewski, Mildred, **31,** 43–44
Sovulewski, Rose, 39, 43, 105
Sovulewski, Tom, 42–44, **45**
Sproat, Florantha, 1–2, 4–5, 7
Stein, Gertrude, 61
Stewart Indian School, 63
Stoddard, Charles Warren, 3
Stoneman House, 13, 17–18, 24, 30, 38
Storch, Kenny, 92, 94
Storch, Lee, 92
Storch, Mary, 92
Strentzel, John T., 46
Sturm, Dr. Avery, 86, 101
Swan, Frank, 92, 96
Swan, Georgie, 92
Swan, Glendon, 91–92, 96

T

Tabuce
    See Howard, Maggie
Tarnutzer, Gayle, 78, **102**
Tatch, Kittie, 29
Taylor, Lawrence, 44
Taylor, Margaret Anne, 44, 97
Taylor, Nancy, 45
Telles family, 11
Telles, John, **79,** 97
Telles, Lucy, 67, 69
Temple, Shirley, **88,** 89
Tenaya Canyon, 50
Thomas, William, 18
Thomson, Charles Goff, 71, 81, 89
Tioga Pass, 96
Tioga Road, 41, 70, 91–92, 94
Toboggan Slide, 79

Tom, Louisa, 82
Townsley, Forrest, 41, 43, 59, 61, 90, 105
Townsley, John, 78, **103,** 105
Tresidder, Don, 67–69, 84–85, 88–89, 98
Tresidder, Mary Curry, 84, 89
Tucker, Eugene, **31**
Tucker, Evelyn, **31**
Tuolumne Grove of Big Trees, 55
Tuolumne Meadows, 50–51, 53, 91–92,
    93, 94–95

U

U. S. Cavalry, 33, 40, 62
Up-ski, 80, **99**
Upper Hotel, 1

V

Van Housen, Barbara, 79, 97
Victory Gardens, 98

W

Waddington, Bette, 75–76
Wagner, Beverly, 75, 101, **104**
Wagner, Bob, 97
Wagner, Jim, 75, 101
Washburn family, 61
Washburn, Albert Henry, 20, 33
Washburn, Clarence, 23
Washburn, Jean Bruce, 20, 21
Washburn, John, 12, 21, 23
Washburn, Wawona, 61
WAVES, 97
Wawona, 19–20, 23, 31, 33, 61, 81, 98
Wawona Grammar School, 22
Wawona Hotel, 7, 12, 20–**21,** 23, 33, 35
Wawona Road, 5, 15, 48, 70, 84
Wawona Tunnel, 70
Webb, Eddie, 67
Wilder, Jane T., 102
Wilkinson, Art, 60, **62**
Wilkinson, Bob, 60

Wilkinson, Clayton, 60
Williams, Bobby, 68
Williams, Marjorie Jane, 68
Wilson, Herbert Earl, 58–59, 69
Womacks, the, 78
Women's Army Corps (WAC), 97
Works Progress Administration
    (WPA), 70
Wosky, Joan, 74, **104**
Wosky, John, 81

Y

Yelverton, Therese, 4
Yosemite Badgers, 78
Yosemite Chapel, 6–7, **10,** 29, 40
    dedication, 9
Yosemite Elementary School, 11, **12,** 15,
    18, 42, 60
    new 1917, 72, 74, 78, 81, 101, 105
    pictures of, **12, 18, 75**
Yosemite Falls Hotel, 17
Yosemite Falls Studio, 36
Yosemite Grant, 3, 5, 20, 26, 38
Yosemite Lodge, 71, 88, 101
Yosemite National Park Company, 42
Yosemite Park and Curry Co., 44, 58,
    60, 63, 69, 74, 78, 81–83,
    86, 97–98, 101, 103, 105
Yosemite Stage & Turnpike Company,
    33
Yosemite Valley Commissioners, 3, 5,
    11, 13–14, 16–17, 26, 30, 33, 35
Yosemite Valley Chapel, 42
Yosemite Valley Railroad, 19, 33, 41
Yosemite Valley Railroad Company, 36
Yosemite Village, 36
Yosemite Zoo, 75

Z

Zaepffel, Annette, 78, 101–102

You can order additional copies of this book directly from the publisher.

Flying Spur Press
P.O. Box 278
Yosemite, CA 95389

Price:—**$14.95.**
Please add **$2.00** for shipping and handling for one book, and **50 cents** for each additional book.
California addresses please add the appropriate sales tax.

Text typeface: Palatino 10/13
Text paper: 60# Glatfelter B–16, acid-free
Printing and binding by BookCrafters, Chelsea, Michigan